AF514143

Tucholsky Wagner Zola Scott Sydow Schlegel
Turgenev Wallace Fonatne Freud
Twain Walther von der Vogelweide Fouqué Friedrich II. von Preußen
Weber Freiligrath Frey
Fechner Fichte Weiße Rose von Fallersleben Kant Ernst Richthofen Frommel
Hölderlin
Fehrs Engels Faber Fielding Flaubert Eichendorff Tacitus Dumas
Eliasberg Ebner Eschenbach
Feuerbach Maximilian I. von Habsburg Fock Eliot Zweig
Ewald Vergil
Goethe Elisabeth von Österreich London
Mendelssohn Balzac Shakespeare Dostojewski Ganghofer
Lichtenberg Rathenau
Trackl Stevenson Doyle Gjellerup
Mommsen Tolstoi Lenz Hambruch
Thoma Hanrieder Droste-Hülshoff
Dach Verne von Arnim Hägele Hauff Humboldt
Reuter
Karrillon Garschin Rousseau Hagen Hauptmann Gautier
Damaschke Defoe Hebbel Baudelaire
Descartes
Wolfram von Eschenbach Schopenhauer Hegel Kussmaul Herder
Bronner Darwin Dickens Melville Grimm Jerome Rilke George
Campe Horváth Aristoteles Bebel Proust
Bismarck Vigny Barlach Voltaire Federer Herodot
Gengenbach Heine
Storm Casanova Lessing Tersteegen Gilm Grillparzer Georgy
Chamberlain Langbein Gryphius
Brentano Lafontaine
Strachwitz Claudius Schiller Kralik Iffland Sokrates
Katharina II. von Rußland Bellamy Schilling
Gerstäcker Raabe Gibbon Tschechow
Löns Hesse Hoffmann Gogol Wilde Gleim Vulpius
Luther Heym Hofmannsthal Klee Hölty Morgenstern
Roth Heyse Klopstock Kleist Goedicke
Luxemburg Puschkin Homer Mörike
La Roche Horaz Musil
Machiavelli Kierkegaard Kraft Kraus
Navarra Aurel Musset
Nestroy Marie de France Lamprecht Kind Kirchhoff Hugo Moltke
Laotse Ipsen Liebknecht
Nietzsche Marx Nansen
von Ossietzky Lassalle Gorki Klett Leibniz Ringelnatz
May vom Stein Lawrence Irving
Petalozzi Platon Knigge
Sachs Poe Pückler Michelangelo Liebermann Kock Kafka
de Sade Praetorius Mistral Zetkin Korolenko

The Reconstructed School

Francis B. Pearson

Imprint

This book is part of the TREDITION CLASSICS series.

Author: Francis B. Pearson
Cover design: toepferschumann, Berlin (Germany)

Publisher: tredition GmbH, Hamburg (Germany)
ISBN: 978-3-8491-8660-9

www.tredition.com
www.tredition.de

Preface

In our school processes there are many constants which have general recognition as such by thoughtful people. On the other hand, there are many variables which should be subjected to close scrutiny to the end that they may be made to yield forth the largest possible returns upon the investment of time and effort. These phases of school procedure constitute the real problem in the work of reconstruction, and the following pages represent an effort to point the way toward larger and better results in the realm of these variables. In general, the aims and purposes of the worker determine the quality of the work done. If, therefore, this volume succeeds in stimulating teachers to elevate the goals of their endeavors, it will have accomplished its purpose.—F.B.P.

Contents

The Reconstructed School

Chapter One

A Preliminary Survey of the Task Before the School

Return to Table of Contents

When people come to think alike, they tend to act alike; unison in thinking begets unison in action. It is often said that the man and wife who have spent years together have grown to resemble each other; but the resemblance is probably in actions rather than in looks; the fact is that they have had common goals of thinking throughout the many years they have lived together and so have come to act in unison. The wise teacher often adjusts difficult situations in her school by inducing the pupils to think toward a common goal. In their zeal for a common enterprise the children forget their differences and attain unison in action as the result of their unison in thinking. The school superintendent knows full well that if he can bring teachers, pupils, and parents to think toward a common goal, he will soon have unity of action. When people catch step mentally, they do the same physically, and as they move forward along the paths of their common thinking, their ways converge until, in time, they find themselves walking side by side in amiable and agreeable converse.

In the larger world outside the school, community enterprises help to generate unity of thinking and consequent unity of action. The pastor finds it one of his larger tasks to establish a focus for the thinking of [2]his people in order to induce concerted action. If the enterprise is one of charity, the neighbors soon find themselves vying with one another in zeal and good will. In the zest of a common purpose they see one another with new eyes and find delight in working with people whose society they once avoided. They can now do teamwork, because they are all thinking toward the same high and worthy goal; lines of demarcation are obliterated and spirits blend in a common purpose. Unity of action becomes inevitable as soon as thinking becomes unified.

Coöperation follows close upon the heels of community thinking. In the presence of a great calamity, rivalries, differences of creed and party, and long-established animosities disappear in the zeal for beneficent action. In the case of fire or flood people are at one in their actions because they are thinking toward the common goal of rescue. They act together only when they think together. Indeed, coöperation is an impossibility apart from unified thinking. Herein lies the efficacy of leadership. It is the province of the leader to induce unity of thinking, to animate with a common purpose, knowing that united action will certainly ensue. If he can cause the thinking of people to center upon a focal point, he establishes his claim to leadership.

What is true of individuals is true, also, of nations. Before they can act in concert, they must think in concert, and, to do this, they must acquire the ability to think toward common goals. If, to illustrate, all nations should come to think toward the goal of democracy, there would ensue a closer sympathy among them, and, in time, modifications of their forms of government would come about as a natural [3]result of their unity of thinking. Again, if all nations of the world should set up the quality of courage as one of the objectives of their thinking they would be drawn closer together in their feelings and in their conduct. If the parents and teachers of all these nations should strive to exorcise fear in the training of children, this purpose would constitute a bond of sympathy among them and they would be encouraged by the reflection that this high purpose was animating parents and teachers the world around. Courage, of course, is of the spirit and typifies many spiritual qualities that characterize civilization of high grade. It is quite conceivable that these qualities of the spirit may become the goals of thinking in all lands. Thus the nations would be brought into a relation of closer harmony. Had a score of boys shared the experience of the lad who grew into the likeness of the Great Stone Face, their differences and disparities would have disappeared in the zeal of a common purpose and they would have become a unified organization in thinking toward the same goal.

We cannot hope to achieve the brotherhood of man until the nations of the world have directed their thinking toward the same goals. What these goals shall be must be determined by competent leadership through the process of education. When we think in unison we are taken out of ourselves and become merged in the spirit of the goal toward which we are thinking. If we were to agree upon courage as one of the spiritual qualities that should characterize all nations and organize all educational forces for the development of this quality, we should find the nations coming closer to one another with this quality as a common possession. Courage gives freedom, and in this freedom the [4]nations would touch spiritual elbows and would thus become spiritual confederates and comrades. By generating and developing this and other spiritual qualities the nations would become merged and unity of feeling and actions would surely ensue. Since love is the greatest thing in the world, this quality may well be made the major goal toward which the thinking of all nations shall be directed. When all peoples come to think and yearn toward this goal, hatred and strife will be banished and peace and righteousness will be enthroned in the hearts of men. When there has been developed in all the nations of the earth an ardent love for the true, the beautiful, and the good, civilization will step up to a higher level and we shall see the dawn of unity.

We who are indulging in dreams of the brotherhood of man must enlarge our concept of society before we can hope to have our dreams come true. It is a far cry from society as a strictly American affair to society as a world affair. The teaching of our schools has had a distinct tendency to restrict our notion of society to that within our own national boundaries. In this we convict ourselves of provincialism. Society is far larger than America, or China, or Russia, or all the islands of the sea in combination. It may entail some straining at the mental leash to win this concept of society, but it must be won as a condition precedent to a fair and just estimate of what the function of education really is and what it is of which the schoolhouse must be an exponent. Society must be thought of as including all nations, tribes, and tongues. In our thinking, the word "society" must suggest the hut that nestles on the mountain-side as well as the palace that fronts the stately boulevard. It must suggest [5]the cape that indents the sea as well as the vast plain that stretches out from river to river. And it must suggest the toiler at his task, the employer at his desk, the man of leisure in his home, the voyager on the ocean, the soldier in the ranks, the child at his lessons, and the mother crooning her baby to sleep.

We descant volubly upon the subjects of citizenship and civilization but, as yet, have achieved no adequate definition of either of the terms upon which we expatiate so fluently. Our books teem with admonitions to train for citizenship in order that we may attain civilization of better quality. But, in all this, we imply American citizenship and American civilization, and here, again, we show forth our provincialism. But even in this restricted field we arrive at our hazy concept of a good citizen by the process of elimination. We aver that a good citizen does not do this and does not do that; yet the teachers in our schools would find it difficult to describe a good citizen adequately, in positive terms. Our notions of good citizenship are more or less vague and misty and, therefore, our concept of civilization is equally so.

Granting, however, that we may finally achieve satisfactory definitions of citizenship and civilization as applying to our own country, it does not follow that the same definitions will obtain in other lands. A good citizen according to the Chinese conception may differ widely from a good citizen in the United States. Topography, climate, associations, occupations, traditions, and racial tendencies must all be taken into account in formulating a definition. Before we can gain a right concept of good citizenship as a world affair we must make a thoughtful study of world conditions. In so doing, we may have occasion to modify and correct [6]some of our own preconceived notions and thus extend the horizon of our education.

What society is and should be in the world at large; what good citizenship is and ought to be in the whole world; and what civilization is, should be, and may be as a world enterprise—these considerations are the foundation stones upon which we must build the temple of education now in the process of reconstruction. Otherwise the work will be narrow, illiberal, spasmodic, and sporadic. It must be possible to arrive at a common denominator of the concepts of society, citizenship, and civilization as pertaining to all nations; it must be possible to contrive a composite of all these concepts to which all nations will subscribe; and it must be possible to discover some fundamental principles that will constitute a focal point toward which the thinking of all nations can be directed. Once this focal point is determined and the thinking of the world focused upon it, the work of reconstruction has been inaugurated.

But the task is not a simple one by any means; quite the contrary, for it is world-embracing in its scope. However difficult the task, it is, none the less, altogether alluring and worthy. It is quite within the range of possibilities for a book to be written, even a textbook, that would serve a useful purpose and meet a distinct need in the schools of all lands. At this point the question of languages obtrudes itself. When people think in unison a common language is reduced to the plane of a mere convenience, not a necessity. The buyer and the seller may not speak the same language but, somehow, they contrive to effect a satisfactory adjustment because their thinking is centered upon the same objective. When thinking becomes cosmopolitan, [7]conduct becomes equally so. If this be conceded, then it is quite within the range of possibilities to formulate a course of study for all the schools of the world, if only we set up as goals the qualities that will make for the well-being of people in all lands. True, the means may differ in different lands, but, even so, the ends will remain constant. A thousand people may set out from their homes with Rome as their destination. They will use all means of travel and speak many languages as they journey forward, but their destination continues constant and they will use the best means at their command to attain the common goal. Similarly, if we set up the quality of loyalty as one of our educational goals, the means may differ but the goal does not change and, therefore, the nations will be actuated by a common purpose in their educational endeavors.

The one thing needful for the execution of this ambitious program of securing concerted thinking is to have in our schools teachers who are world-minded, who think in world units. Such teachers, and only such, can plan for world education and world affairs, and bring their plans to a successful issue. Some teachers seem able to think only of a schoolroom; others of a building; others of a town or township; still others of a state; some of a country; and fewer yet of the world as a single thing. A person can be no larger than his unit of thinking. One who thinks in small units convicts himself of provincialism and soon becomes intolerant. Such a person arrogates to himself superiority and inclines to feel somewhat contemptuous of people outside the narrow limits of his thinking. If he thinks his restricted horizon bounds all that is worth knowing, he will not exert himself to [8]climb to a higher level in order that he may gain a wider view. He is disdainful and intolerant of whatever lies beyond his horizon, and his attitude, if not his words, repeats the question of the culpable Cain, "Am I my brother's keeper?" He is encased in an armor that is impervious to ordinary appeal. He is satisfied with himself and asks merely to be let alone. He is quite content to be held fast bound in his traditional moorings without any feeling of sympathy for the world as a whole.

The reverse side of the picture reveals the teacher who is world-minded. Such a teacher is never less than magnanimous; intolerance has no place in his scheme of life; he is in sympathy with all nations in their progress toward light and right; and he is interested in all world progress whether in science, in art, in literature, in economics, in industry, or in education. To this end he is careful to inform himself as to world movements and notes with keen interest the trend and development of civilization. Being a world-citizen himself, he strives, in his school work, to develop in his pupils the capacity and the desire for world-citizenship. With no abatement of thoroughness in the work of his school, he still finds time to look up from his tasks to catch the view beyond his own national boundaries. If the superintendent who is world-minded has the hearty coöperation of teachers who are also world-minded, together they will be able to develop a plan of education that is world-wide. To produce teachers of this type may require a readjustment and reconstruction of the work of colleges and training schools to the end that the teachers they send forth may measure up to the requirements of this world-wide concept of education. But these institutions can hardly hope to be immune to the process [9]of reconstruction. They can hardly hope to cite the past as a guide for the future, for traditional lines are being obliterated and new lines are being marked out for civilization, including education in its larger and newer import.

[10]

Chapter Two

The Past as Related to the Present

Return to Table of Contents

In a significant degree the present is the heritage of the past, and any critical appraisement of the present must take cognizance of the influence of the past. That there are weak places in our present civilization, no one will deny; nor will it be denied that the sources of some of these may be found in the past. We have it on good authority that "the fathers have eaten sour grapes and the children's teeth are set on edge." Had the eating of sour grapes in the past been more restricted, the present generation would stand less in need of dentistry. When we take an inventory of the people of the present who are defective in body, in mind, or in spirit, it seems obvious that the consumption of sour grapes, in the past, must have been quite extensive. If the blood of the grandfather was tainted, it is probable that the blood of the grandchild is impure.

The defects of the present would seem to constitute a valid indictment against the educational agencies of the past. These agencies are not confined to the school but include law, medicine, civics, sociology, government, hygiene, eugenics, home life, and physical training. Had all these phases of education done their perfect work in the past, the present would be in better case. It seems a great pity that it required a world war to render us conscious of many of the defects of society. The draft board made discoveries of facts that seem to have eluded the home, the school, the family physician, and the boards of health. Many of these discoveries are most disquieting and reflect unfavorably upon some of the educational practices of [11]the past. The many cases of physical unfitness and the fewer cases of athletic hearts seem to have escaped the attention of physical directors and athletic coaches, not to mention parents and physicians. Seeing that one fourth of our young men have been pronounced physically unsound, it behooves us to turn our gaze toward the past to determine, if possible, wherein our educational processes have been at fault.

The thoughtful person who stands on the street-corner watching the promiscuous throng pass by and making a careful appraisement of their physical, mental, and spiritual qualities, will not find the experience particularly edifying. He will note many facts that will depress rather than encourage and inspire. In the throng he will see many men and women, young and old, who, as specimens of physical manhood and womanhood, are far from perfect. He will see many who are young in years but who are old in looks and physical bearing. They creep or shuffle along as if bowed down with the weight of years, lacking the graces of buoyancy and abounding youth. They are bent, gnarled, shriveled, faded, weak, and wizened. Their faces reveal the absence of the looks that betoken hope, courage, aspiration, and high purpose. Their lineaments and their gait show forth a ghastly forlornness that excites pity and despair. They seem the veriest derelicts, tossed to and fro by the currents of life without hope of redemption.

Their whole bearing indicates that they are languid, morbid, misanthropic, and nerveless. They seem ill-nourished as well as mentally and spiritually starved. They seem the victims of inherited or acquired weaknesses that stamp them as belonging among the physically unfit. If the farmer should discover among his [12]animals as large a percentage of unfitness and imperfection, he would reach the conclusion at once that something was radically wrong and would immediately set on foot well-thought-out plans to rectify the situation. But, seeing that these derelicts are human beings and not farm stock, we bestow upon them a sneer, or possibly a pittance by way of alms, and pass on our complacent ways. Looking upon the imperfect passersby, the observer is reminded of the tens of thousands of children who are defective in mind and body and are hidden away from public gaze, a charge upon the resources of the state.

Such a setting forth of the less agreeable side of present conditions would seem out of place, if not actually impertinent, were we inclined to ignore the fact that diagnosis must precede treatment. The surgeon knows full well that there will be pain, but he is comforted by the reflection that restoration to health will succeed the pain. We need to look squarely at the facts as they are in order to determine what must be done to avert a repetition in the future. We have seen the sins of the fathers visited upon the children to the third and fourth generation and still retained our complacency. We preach temperance to the young men of our day, but fail to set forth the fact that right living on their part will make for the well-being of their grandchildren. We exhibit our thoroughbred live stock at our fairs and plume ourselves upon our ability to produce stock of such quality. In the case of live stock we know that the present is the product of the past, but seem less ready to acknowledge the same fact as touching human animals. We may know that our ancestors planted thorns and yet we seem surprised that we cannot gather a harvest of grapes, and we [13]would fain gather figs from a planting of thistles. But this may not be. We harvest according to the planting of our ancestors, and, with equal certainty, if we eat sour grapes the teeth of our descendants will surely be put on edge.

If we are to reconstruct our educational processes we must make a critical survey of the entire situation that we may be fully advised of the magnitude of the problem to which we are to address ourselves. We may not blink the facts but must face them squarely; otherwise we shall not get on. We may take unction to ourselves for our philanthropic zeal in caring for our unfortunates in penal and eleemosynary institutions, but that will not suffice. We must frankly consider by what means the number of these unfortunates may be reduced. If we fail to do this we convict ourselves of cowardice or impotence. We pile up our millions in buildings for the insane, the feeble-minded, the vicious, the epileptic, and plume ourselves upon our munificence. But if all these unfortunates could be redeemed from their thralldom, and these countless millions turned back into the channels of trade, civilization would take on a new meaning. Here is one of the problems that calls aloud to education for a solution and will not be denied.

One of the avowed purposes of education is to lift society to a higher plane of thinking and acting, and it is always and altogether pertinent to make an inventory to discover if this laudable purpose is being accomplished. Such an inventory can be made only by an analyst; the work cannot be delegated either to a pessimist or to an optimist. In his efforts to determine whether society is advancing or receding, the analyst often makes disquieting discoveries.

[14] It must be admitted by the most devoted and patriotic American that our civilization includes many elements that can truly be denominated frivolous, superficial, artificial, and inconsequential. As a people, we seek to be entertained, but fail to make a nice distinction between entertainment and amusement. War, it is true, has caused us to think more soberly and feel more deeply; but the bizarre, the gaudy, and the superficial still make a strong appeal to us. We are quite happy to wear paste diamonds, provided only that they sparkle. So long have we been substituting the fictitious for the genuine that we have contracted the habit of loose, fictitious thinking. So much does the show element appeal to us that we incline to parade even our troubles. Simplicity and sincerity, whether in dress, in speech, or in conduct, have so long been foreign to our daily living and thinking that we incline to style these qualities as old-fogyish.

A hundred or more young men came to a certain city to enlist for the war. As they marched out through the railway station they rent the air with whooping and yells and other manifestations of boisterous conduct. These young fellows may have hearts of gold, but their real manhood was overlaid with a veneer of rudeness that could not commend them to the admiration of cultivated persons. Inside the station was another group of young men in khaki who were quiet, dignified, and decorous. The contrast between the two groups was most striking, and the bystanders were led to wonder whether it requires a world-war to teach our young men manners and whether the schools and homes have abdicated in favor of the cantonment in the teaching of deportment. In the schools and the homes that are to be in our good land we may well hope that [15]decorum will be emphasized and magnified; for decorum is evermore the fruitage of intellectuality and genuine culture.

As a nation, we have been prodigal of our resources and, especially, of our time. We have failed to regard our leisure hours as a liability but, like the lotus eaters, have dallied in the realm of pleasure. Like children at play, we have gone on our pleasure-seeking ways all heedless of the clock, and, when misfortune came and necessity arose, many of us were unwilling and more of us unable to engage in the work of production. In some localities legislation was invoked to urge us toward the fields and gardens. We have shown ourselves a wasteful people, and in the wake of our wastefulness have followed a dismal train of disasters, cold, hunger, and many another form of distress. Deplore and repent of our prodigality as we may, the effects abide to remind us of our decline from the high plane of industry, frugality, and conservation of leisure. Nor can we hope to avert a repetition of this crisis unless education comes in to guide our minds and hands aright.

Again, we have been wont to estimate men by what they have rather than by what they are, and to regard as of value only such things as are quoted in the markets. Wall Street takes precedence over the university and to the millionaire we accord the front seat even in some of our churches. We accept the widow's mite but do not inscribe her name upon the roll of honor. We give money prizes for work in our schools and thus strive to commercialize the things of the mind and of the spirit. We have laid waste our forests, impoverished our fields, and defiled our landscapes to stimulate [16]increased activity in our clearing-houses. Like Jason of old, we have wandered far in quest of the golden fleece. We welcome the rainbow, not for its beauty but for the bag of gold at its end. We seek to scale the heights of Olympus by stairways of gold, fondly nursing the conceit that, once we have scaled these heights, we shall be equal to the gods.

To indulge in even such a brief review of some of the weak places and defections of society is not an agreeable task, but diagnosis must necessarily precede the application of remedies. If we are to reconstruct education in order to effect a reconstruction of society we must know our problem in advance, that we may proceed in a rational way. Reconstruction cannot be made permanently effective by haphazard methods. We must visualize clearly the objectives of our endeavors in order to obviate wrong methods and futility. We must have the whole matter laid bare before our eyes or we shall not get on in the work of reconstruction. It were more agreeable to dwell upon our achievements, and they are many, but the process of reconstruction has to do with the affected parts. These must be our special care, these the realm for our kindly surgery and the arts of healing. We need to become acutely conscious that the present will become the past and that there will be a new present which will take on the same qualities that now characterize our present. We need to feel that the future will look back to our present and commend or condemn according to the practices of this generation. And the only way to make a sane and right future is to create a sane and right present.

[17]

Chapter Three

The Future as Related to the Present

Return to Table of Contents

In planning a journey the one constant is the destination. All the other elements are variable, and, therefore, subordinate. So, also, in planning a course of study. The qualities to be developed through the educational processes are the constants, while the agencies by which these qualities are to be attained are subject to change. The course of study provides for the school activities for the child for a period of twelve years, and it is altogether pertinent to inquire what qualities we hope to develop by means of these school activities. To do this effectively we must visualize the pupil when he emerges from the school period and ask ourselves what qualities we hope to have him possess at the close of this period. If we decide upon such qualities as imagination, initiative, aspiration, appreciation, courage, loyalty, reverence, a sense of responsibility, integrity, and serenity, we have discovered some of the constants toward which all the work of the twelve years must be directed. In planning a course of study toward these constants we do not restrict the scope of the pupil's activities; quite the reverse. We thus enlarge the concept of education both for himself and his teachers and emphasize the fact that education is a continuous process and may not be marked by grades or subjects. For the teachers we establish goals of school endeavor and thus unify and articulate all their efforts. We focus their attention upon the pupil as they would all wish to see him when he completes the work of the school.

If children are asked why they go to school, nine [18]out of ten, perhaps, will reply that they go to school to learn arithmetic, grammar, geography, and history. Asked what their big purpose is in teaching, probably three out of five teachers will answer that they are actuated by a desire to cause their pupils to know arithmetic, grammar, geography, and history. One of the other five teachers may echo something out of her past accumulations to the effect that her work is the training for citizenship, and the fifth will say quite frankly that she is groping about, all the while, searching for the answer to that very question. It would be futile to ask the children why they desire knowledge of these subjects and there might be hazard in propounding the same question to the three teachers. They teach arithmetic because it is in the course of study; it is in the course of study because the superintendent put it there; and the superintendent put it there because some other superintendent has it in his course of study.

Now arithmetic may, in reality, be one of the best things a child can study; but the child takes it because the teacher prescribes it, and the teacher takes it on faith because the superintendent takes it on faith and she cannot go counter to the dictum of the superintendent. Besides, it is far easier to teach arithmetic than it would be to challenge the right of this subject to a place in the course of study. To most people, including many teachers, arithmetic is but a habit of thinking. They have been contracting this habit through all the years since the beginning of their school experience, until now it seems as inevitable as any other habitual affair. It is quite as much a habit of their thinking as eating, sleeping, or walking. If there were no arithmetic, they argue subconsciously, [19]there could be no school; for arithmetic and school are synonymous. Again, let it be said that there is no thought here of inveighing against arithmetic or any other subject of the curriculum. Not arithmetic in itself, but the arithmetic habit constitutes the incubus, the evil spirit that needs to be exorcised.

This arithmetic habit had its origin, doubtless, in the traditional concept of knowledge as power. An adage is not easily controverted or eradicated. The copy-books of the fathers proclaimed boldly that knowledge is power, and the children accepted the dictum as inviolable. If it were true that knowledge is power, the procedure of the schools and the course of conduct of the teachers during all these years would have ample justification. The entire process would seem simplicity itself. So soon as we acquire knowledge we should have power—and power is altogether desirable. The trouble is that we have been confusing knowledge and wisdom in the face of the poet's declaration that "Knowledge and wisdom, far from being one, have ofttimes no connection." Our experience should have taught us that many people who have much knowledge are relatively impotent for the reason that they have not learned how to use their knowledge in the way of generating power. Gasoline is an inert substance, but, under well-understood conditions, it affords power. Water is not power, but man has learned how to use it in generating power. Knowledge is convenient and serviceable, but its greatest utility lies in the fact that it can be employed in producing power.

We are prone to take our judgments ready-made and have been relying upon the copy-books of the fathers rather than our own reasoning powers. If we had only learned in childhood the distinction between knowledge [20]and wisdom; if we had learned that knowledge is not power but merely potential; and if we had learned that knowledge is but the means to an end and not the end itself, we should have been spared many a delusion and our educational sky would not now be so overcast with clouds. We have been proceeding upon the agreeable assumption that arithmetic, geography, and history are the goals of every school endeavor, the Ultima Thule of every educational quest. The child studies arithmetic, is subjected to an examination that may represent the bent or caprice of the teacher, manages to struggle through seventy per cent of the answers, is promoted to the next higher grade, and, thereupon, starts on his journey around another circle. And we call this education. These processes constitute the mechanics of education, but, in and of themselves, they are not education. One of the big problems of the school today is to emancipate both teachers and pupils from the erroneous notion that they are.

The child does not go to school to learn arithmetic and spelling and grammar. The goal to be attained is far higher and better than either of these or all combined. The study of arithmetic may prove a highly profitable means, never the end to be gained. This statement will be boldly challenged by the traditional teacher, but it is so strongly intrenched in logic and sound pedagogy that it is impregnable. The goal might, possibly, be reached without the aid of arithmetic, but, if a knowledge of this subject will facilitate the process, then, of course, it becomes of value and should be used. Let us assume, for the moment, that the teacher decides to set up thoroughness as one of the large objectives of her teaching. While she may be able to reach this goal sooner by means of arithmetic, [21]no one will contend that arithmetic is indispensable. Nor, indeed, will any one contend that arithmetic is comparable to thoroughness as a goal to be attained. If the teacher's constant aim is thoroughness, she will achieve even better results in the arithmetic and will inculcate habits in her pupils that serve them in good stead throughout life. For the quality of thoroughness is desirable in every activity of life, and we do well to emphasize every study and every activity of the school that helps in the development of this quality.

If the superintendent were challenged to adduce a satisfactory reason why he has not written thoroughness into his course of study he might be hard put to it to justify the omission. He hopes, of course, that the quality of thoroughness will issue somehow from the study of arithmetic and science, but he lacks the courage, apparently, to proclaim this hope in print. He says that education is a spiritual process, while his course of study proves that he is striving to produce mental acrobats, relegating the spiritual qualities to the rank of by-products. His course of study shows conclusively that he thinks that knowledge is power. Once disillusion him on this point and his course of study will cease to be to him the sacrosanct affair it has always appeared and he will no longer look upon it as a sort of sacrilege to inject into this course of study some elements that seem to violate the sanctities of tradition.

Advancing another brief step, we may try to imagine the superintendent's suggesting to the teachers at the opening of the school year that they devote the year to inculcating in their pupils the qualities of thoroughness, self-control, courage, and reverence. The faces of the teachers, at such a proposal, would undoubtedly afford [22]opportunity for an interesting study and the linguistic reactions of some of them would be forcible to the point of picturesqueness. The traditional teachers would demand to know by what right he presumed to impose upon them such an unheard-of program. Others might welcome the suggestion as a means of relief from irritating and devastating drudgery. In their quaint innocence and guilelessness their souls would revel in rainbow dreams of preachments, homilies, and wise counsel that would cause the qualities of self-control and reverence to spring into being full-grown even as Minerva from the head of Jove.

But their beatific visions would dissolve upon hearing the superintendent name certain teachers to act as a committee to determine and report upon the studies that would best serve the purpose of generating reverence, and another committee to select the studies that would most effectively stimulate and develop self-control, and so on through the list. It is here that we find the crux of the whole matter. Here the program collides with tradition and with stereotyped habits of thinking. Many superintendents and teachers will contend that such a problem is impossible of solution because no one has ever essayed such a task. No one, they argue, has ever determined what subjects will effectually generate the specific qualities self-control or reverence, no one has ever discovered what school studies will function in given spiritual qualities. According to their course of reasoning nothing is possible that has not already been done. However, there are some progressive, dynamic superintendents and teachers who will welcome the opportunity to test their resourcefulness in seeking the solution of a problem that is both new and big. To these dynamic ones we must look [23]for results and when this solution is evolved, the work of reconstruction will move on apace.

Reverting, for the moment, to the subject of thoroughness: it must be clear that this quality is worthy a place in the course of study because it is worthy the best efforts of the pupil. Furthermore, it is worthy the best efforts of the pupil because it is an important element of civilization. These statements all need reiteration and emphasis to the end that they may become thoroughly enmeshed in the social consciousness. If we can cause people to think toward thoroughness rather than toward arithmetic or other school studies, we shall win the feeling that we are making progress. Thoroughness must be distinguished, of course, from a smattering knowledge of details that have no value. In the right sense thoroughness must be interpreted as the habit of mastery. We may well indulge the hope that the time will come when parents will invoke the aid of the schools to assist their children in acquiring this habit of mastery. When that time comes the schools will be working toward larger and higher objectives and education will have become a spiritual process in reality.

It will be readily conceded that the habit of mastery is a desirable quality in every vocation and in every avocation. It is a very real asset on the farm, in the factory, in legislative halls, in the offices of lawyer and physician, in the study, in the shop, and in the home. When mastery becomes habitual with people in all these activities society will thrill with the pulsations of new life and civilization will rise to a higher level. But how may the child acquire this habit of mastery? On what meat shall this our pupil feed that he may become master of himself, master of all his powers, and master [24]of every situation in which he finds himself? How shall he win that mastery that will enable him to interpret every obstacle as a new challenge to his powers, and to translate temporary defeat into ultimate victory? How may he enter into such complete sense of mastery that he will not quail in the presence of difficulties, that he will never display the white flag or the white feather, that he will ever show forth the spirit of Henley's *Invictus*, and that nothing short of death may avail to absolve him from his obligations to his high standards?

These questions are referred, with all proper respect, to the superintendent, the principal, and the teachers, whose province it is to vouchsafe satisfactory answers. If they tell us that arithmetic will be of assistance in the way of inculcating this habit of mastery, then we shall hail arithmetic with joyous acclaim and accord it a place of honor in the school regime,—but only as an auxiliary, only as a means to the great end of mastery. If they assure us that science will be equally serviceable in our enterprise of developing mastery, then we shall give to science an equally hearty welcome. However, we shall emphasize the right to stipulate that, in the course of study, the capitals shall be reserved for the big objective thoroughness, of the habit of mastery, and that the means be given in small letters and as sub-heads.

We may indulge in the conceit that a flag floats at the summit of a lofty and more or less rugged elevation. The youth who essays the task of reaching that flag will need to reinforce his strength at supply stations along the way. If we style one of these stations arithmetic, it will be evident, at once, that this station is a subsidiary element in the enterprise and not the [25]goal, for that is the flag at the top. These supply stations are useful in helping the youth to reach his goal. We may conceive of many of these stations, such as algebra, or history, or Greek, or Chinese. Whatever their names, they are all but means to an end and when that end has been attained the youth can afford to forget them, in large part, save only in gratitude for their help in enabling him to win the goal of thoroughness.

The child eats beefsteak because it is palatable; the mother prescribes beefsteak and prepares it carefully with the child's health as the goal of her interests. Moreover, she has a more vital interest in beefsteak because she is thinking of health as the goal. For another child, she may prescribe eggs and, for still another, milk or oatmeal, according to each one's needs. Health is the big goal and these foods are the supply stations along the way. The physician must assist in determining what articles of food will best serve the purpose and to this end he must cooperate with the mother in knowing his patients. He must have knowledge of foods and must know how to adapt means to ends, never losing sight of the real goal. The inference is altogether obvious. A superintendent must write the prescription in the form of a course of study and he may not with impunity mistake a supply station for the goal. He must have knowledge of the pupils and know their individual needs and native interests. Having gained this knowledge, he will supply abundant electives in order to assist each child in the best possible way toward the goal.

If, then, the relation between major ends and minor means has been made clear, we are ready for the statement that these major ends may be made the common [26]goals of endeavor in the schools of all lands. Thoroughness is quite as necessary in the rice fields of China as in the wheat fields of America, as necessary in the banks of Rome as in the banks of New York, quite as essential to mercantile transactions in Cape Town as in Chicago, and quite as essential to home life in Tokyo as in San Francisco. If these big objectives are set up in the schools of all countries pupils, teachers, and people will come to think in unison and thus their ways will converge and they will come to act in unison. The same high purposes will actuate and animate society as a whole and this, in turn, will make for a higher type of civilization and accelerate progress toward unity in school procedure.

[27]

Chapter Four

Integrity

Return to Table of Contents

Integrity connotes many qualities that are necessary to success in the high art of right and rational living and that are conspicuous, therefore, in society of high grade. It is an inclusive quality, and is, in reality, a federation of qualities that are esteemed essential to a highly developed civilization. The term, like the word from which it is derived, *integer*, signifies completeness, wholeness, entirety, soundness, rectitude, unimpaired state. It implies no scarification, no blemish, no unsoundness, no abrasion, no disfigurement, no distortion, no defect. In ordinary parlance integrity and honesty are regarded as synonyms, but a close analysis discovers honesty to be but one of the many manifestations of integrity. Lincoln displayed honesty in returning the pennies by way of rectifying a mistake, but that act, honest as it was, did not engage all his integrity. This big quality manifested itself at Gettysburg, in the letter to Mrs. Bixby, in visiting the hospitals to comfort and cheer the wounded soldiers, and in his magnanimity to those who maligned him.

In every individual the inward quality determines the outward conduct in all its ramifications, whether in his speech, in his actions, or in his attitude toward other individuals. It is quite as true in a pedagogical sense as in the scriptural sense that "Men do not gather grapes of thorns or figs of thistles," and, also, that "By their fruits ye shall know them." The stream does not rise higher than the source. What a man is doing and how he is doing it tells us what [28]he is. When we would appraise a man's character we take note of his habits, his daily walk and conversation in all his relations to his fellows. If we find a blemish in his conduct, we arrive at the judgment that his character is not without blemish. In short, his habitual acts and speech, in the marts of trade, in the office, in the field, in the home, and in the forum betoken the presence or absence of integrity. It follows, then, as a corollary that, if we hope to have in the stream of life that we call society the elements that make for a high type of civilization we must have integrity at the source; and with this quality at the source these elements will inevitably issue forth into the life currents. This being true, we have clear warrant for the affirmation that integrity is a worthy goal toward which we do well to direct the activities of the school.

Integrity in its large import implies physical soundness, mental soundness, and moral soundness. In time we may come to realize that physical soundness and mental soundness are but sequences of moral soundness, or, in other words, that a sound body and a sound mind are manifestations of a right spirit. But, for the present, we may waive this consideration and think of the three phases of integrity—physical, mental and moral. If, at the age of eighteen years, the boy or girl emerges from school experience sound in body, in mind, and in spirit, society will affirm that education has been effective. To develop young persons of this type is a work that is worthy the best efforts of the home, the school, the church and society, nor can any one of these agencies shift or shirk responsibility. The school has a large share of this responsibility, and those whose duty it is to formulate a course of study may well ask themselves what procedure of the school will [29]best assist the child to attain integrity by means of the school activities.

In our efforts to generate this quality of integrity, or, indeed, any quality, it must be kept clearly in mind every day and every hour of the day that the children with whom we have to do are not all alike. On the contrary, they differ, and often differ widely, in respect of mental ability, environment, inheritances, and native disposition. If they were all alike, it would be most unfortunate, but we could treat them all alike in our teaching and so fix and perpetuate their likeness to one another. Some teachers have heard and read a hundred times that our teaching should attach itself to the native tendencies of the child; yet, in spite of this, the teacher proceeds as if all children were alike and all possessed the same native tendencies. Herein lies a part of the tragedy of our traditional, stereotyped, race-track teaching. We assume that children are all alike, that they are standardized children, and so we prescribe for them a standardized diet and serve it by standardized methods. If we were producing bricks instead of embryo men and women our procedure would be laudable, for, in the making of bricks, uniformity is a prime necessity. Each brick must be exactly like every other brick, and, in consequence, we use for each one ingredients of the same quality and in like amount, and then subject them all to precisely the same treatment.

This procedure is well enough in the case of inanimate bricks, but it is far from well enough in the case of animate, sentient human beings. It would be a calamity to have duplicate human beings, and yet the traditional school seems to be doing its utmost to produce duplicates. The native tendencies of one boy impel him [30]toward the realms of nature, but, all heedless of this big fact, we bind him hard and fast to some academic post with traditional bonds of rules and regulations and then strive to coerce him into partaking of our traditional pabulum. His inevitable rebellion against this regime we style incorrigibility, or stupidity, and then by main strength and authority strive to reduce him to submission and, failing in this, we banish him from the school branded for life. Our treatment of this boy is due to the fact that another boy in the school is endowed with other native tendencies and the teacher is striving to fashion both boys in the same mold.

In striving to inculcate the quality of integrity, wholeness, soundness, rectitude in Sam Brown our aim is to develop this specific boy into the best Sam Brown possible and not to try to make of him another Harry Smith. We need one best Sam Brown and one best Harry Smith but not two Harry Smiths. If we try to make our Sam Brown into a second Harry Smith, society is certain to be the loser to the value of Sam Brown. We want to see Sam Brown realize all his possibilities to the utmost, for only so will he win integrity. Better a complete Sam Brown, though only half the size of Harry Smith, than an incomplete Sam Brown of any size. If the native tendencies of Sam Brown lead toward nature, certain it is that by denying him the stimulus of nature study, we shall restrict his growth and render him less than complete. If we would produce a complete Sam Brown, if we would have him attain integrity, we must see to it that the process of teaching engages all his powers and does not permit some of these powers to lie fallow.

If Sam Brown is a nature boy, no amount of coercion [31]can transform him into a mathematics boy. True he may, in time, gain proficiency in mathematics, but only if he is led into the field of mathematics through the gateway of nature. He may ultimately achieve distinction as a writer, but not unless his pen becomes facile in depicting nature. Unless his native interests are taken fully into account and all his powers are enlisted in the enterprise of education toward integrity, he will never become the Sam Brown he might have been and the teacher cannot win special comfort in the reflection that she has helped to produce a cripple. We can better afford to depart from the beaten path, and even do violence to the sanctity of the course of study, than to lose or deform Sam Brown. If his soul yearns for green fields and budding trees, it is cruel if not criminal to fail to cater to this yearning. And only by cultivating and ministering to this native disposition can we hope to be of service in aiding him to achieve integrity.

It needs to be emphasized that integrity signifies one hundred per cent, nothing less, and that such a goal is quite worth working toward. On the physical side, the problem looms large before us. Since we can produce thoroughbred live stock that scores one hundred per cent, we ought to produce one hundred per cent men and women. In a great university, physical examinations covering a period of seventeen years discovered one physically perfect young woman and not one physically perfect young man. Our live stock records make a better showing than this. For years we have been quoting "a sound mind in a sound body" in various languages but have failed in a large degree to achieve sound bodies. Nor, indeed, may we hope to win this goal until we become aroused to the importance [32]of physical training in its widest import for all young people and not merely for the already physically fit, who constitute the ball teams. If the child is physically sound at the age of six, he ought to be no less so at the age of eighteen. If he is not so, there must have been some blundering in the course of his school life, either on the part of the school itself or of the home. When we set up physical soundness as the goal of our endeavors and this ideal becomes enmeshed in the consciousness of all citizens, then activities toward this end will inevitably ensue. Physical training will be made an integral part of the course of study, medical and dental inspection will obtain both in the school and in the home, insanitary conditions will no longer be tolerated, intemperance in every form will disappear, and every child will receive the same careful nurture that we now bestow upon the prize winners at our live-stock exhibition. The thinking of people will be intent toward the one hundred per cent standard and, in consequence, they will strive in unison to achieve this goal.

The large amount of incompleteness that is to be found among the products of our schools may be traced, in a large measure, to our irrational and fictitious procedure in the matter of grading. We must keep records, of course, but it will be recalled that in the parable of the talents men were commended or condemned according to the use they made of the talents they had and were not graded according to a fixed standard. Seeing that seventy-five per cent will win him promotion, the boy devotes only so much of himself to the enterprise as will enable him to attain the goal and directs the remainder of himself to adventures along the line of his native tendencies. The only way [33]by which we can develop a complete Sam Brown is so to arrange matters that the whole of Sam Brown is enlisted in the work. Otherwise we shall have one part of the boy working in one direction and another part in another direction, and that plan does not make for completeness. We must enlist the whole boy or we shall fail to develop a complete boy. If we can find some study to which he will devote himself unreservedly, then we may well rejoice and can afford to let the traditional subjects of the course of study wait. We are interested in Sam Brown just now and he is far more important than some man-made course of study. We are interested, too, in one hundred per cent of Sam Brown, and not in three fourths of him. If arithmetic will not enlist all of this boy and nature will enlist all of him, then arithmetic must be held in abeyance in the interest of the whole boy.

The seventy-five per cent standard is repudiated by the world of affairs even though it is emphasized by the school. Seventy-five per cent of accuracy will not do in the transactions of the bank. The accounts must balance to the penny. The figures are right or else they are wrong. There is no middle ground. In the school the boy solves three problems but fails with the fourth. None the less he wins the goal of promotion. Not so at the bank. He is denied admission because of his failure with the fourth problem. Seventy-five will not do in joining the spans of the great bridge across the river. We must have absolute accuracy if we would avoid a wreck with its attendant horrors. The druggist must not fall below one hundred per cent in compounding the prescription unless he would face a charge of criminal negligence. The wireless operator must transcribe the message with absolute accuracy or dire [34]consequences may ensue. The railway crew must read the order without a mistake if they would save life and property from disaster.

But, in the school, the teachers rejoice and congratulate one another when their pupils achieve a grade of seventy-five. It matters nothing, apparently, that this grade of seventy-five is a fictitious thing with no basis in logic or reason, in short a mere habit that has no justification save in tradition, and that, in very truth, it is a concession to inaccuracy and ignorance. When we promote the boy for solving three out of four problems we virtually say to him that the fourth problem is negligible and he may as well forget all about it. Sometimes a teacher grieves over a grade of seventy-three, never realizing that another teacher might have given to that same paper a grade of eighty-three. We proclaim education to be a spiritual process, and then, in some instances, employ mechanics to administer this process. By what process of reasoning the superintendent or the teacher arrives at the judgment that seventy-five is good enough is yet to be explained. Our zeal for grades and credits indicates a greater interest in the label than in the contents of the package.

Teaching is a noble work if only it is directed toward worthy goals. Nothing in the way of human endeavor can be more inspiring than the work of striving to integrate boys and girls. The mere droning over geography, and history, and grammar is petty by comparison. And yet all these studies and many others may be found essential factors in the work and they will be learned with greater thoroughness as means to a great end than as ends in themselves. The supply stations take on a new meaning to the boy who is [35]yearning to reach the flag at the top. But it needs to be said here that the traditional superintendent and teacher will greet this entire plan with a supercilious smile. They will call it visionary, unpractical, and idealistic—then return to their seventy-five per cent regime with the utmost complacency and self-satisfaction. It is ever so with the traditional teacher. He seeks to be let alone, that he may go on his complacent way without hindrance. To him every innovation is an interference, if not a positive impertinence. But, in spite of the traditional teacher, the school is destined to rise to a higher level and enter upon a more rational procedure. And we must look to the dynamic teacher to usher in the renaissance—the teacher who has the vitality and the courage to break away from tradition and write integrity into the course of study as one of the big goals and think all the while toward integrity, physical, mental, and moral.

[36]

Chapter Five

Appreciation

Return to Table of Contents

Education may be defined as the process of raising the level of appreciation. This definition will stand the ultimate test. Here is bed-rock; here is the foundation upon which we may predicate appreciation as a goal in every rational system of education. Appreciation has been defined as a judgment of values, a feeling for the essential worth of things, and, as such, it lies at the very heart of real education. It must be so or civilization cannot be. Without appreciation there can be no distinction between the coarse and the fine, none between the high and the low, none between the beautiful and the ugly, none between the sublime and the commonplace, none between zenith and nadir. Hence, appreciation is inevitable in every course of study, whether the authorities have the courage to proclaim it or not. Just why it has not been written into the course of study is inexplicable, seeing that it is fundamental in the educational process. It is far from clear why the superintendent permits teachers and pupils to go on their way year after year thinking that arithmetic is their final destination, or why he fails to take the taxpayers into his confidence and explain to them that appreciation is one of the lode-stars toward which the schools are advancing. In his heart he hopes that the schools may achieve appreciation, and it would be the part of frankness and fairness for him to reveal this hope to his teachers and to all others concerned.

It is common knowledge that business affairs do not require more than ten pages of arithmetic and it would [37]seem only fair that the study of the other pages should be justified. These other pages must serve some useful purpose in the thinking of those who retain them, and, certainly, no harm would ensue from a revelation of this purpose. If they are studied as a means to some high end, they will prove no less important after this fact has been explained. We may need more arithmetic than we have, but it is our due to be informed why we need it; to what use it is to be put. These things we have a right to know, and no superintendent, who is charged with the responsibility of making the course of study, has a right to withhold the information. If he does not know the explanation of the course of study he has devised, he ought to make known that fact and throw himself "on the mercy of the court."

In these days of conservation and elimination of waste every subject that seeks admission to the course of study should be challenged at the door and be made to show what useful purpose it is to serve. Nor should any subject be admitted on any specious pretext. If there are subjects that are better adapted to the high purposes of education than the ones we are now using, then, by all means, let us give them a hearty welcome.

Above all, we should be careful not to retain a subject unless it has a more valid passport than old age to justify its retention. If Chinese will help us win the goal of appreciation more effectively than Latin, then, by all means, we should make the substitution. But, in doing so, we must exercise care not to be carried away by a yearning for novelty. Least of all should any subject be admitted to the course of study that does not have behind it something more substantial and enduring than whim or caprice.

The subjects that avail in generating and stimulating [38]the growth of appreciation are many and of great variety. Nor are they all found in the proverbial course of study of the schools. When the boy first really sees an ear of corn from another viewpoint than the economic, he finds it eloquent of the marvelous adaptations of nature. From being a mere ear of corn it becomes a revelation of design and beauty. No change has taken place in the ear of corn, but a most important change has been wrought in the boy. Such a change is so subtle, so delicate, and so intangible that it cannot be measured in terms of per cents; but it is no less real for all that. It is a spiritual process and, therefore, aptly illustrates the accepted definition of education. Though it defies analysis and the rule of thumb, the boy is conscious of it and can say with the man who was born blind, "One thing I know, that, whereas I was blind, now I see," and no cabalistic marks in a grade-book can express the value of the change indicated by that statement.

The sluggard deems the sunrise an impertinence because it disturbs his morning slumber; but such a change may be wrought in him as to cause him to stand in reverence before the very thing he once condemned. The sunrise, once an affront, is now nothing less than a miracle, and he stands in the sublime presence with uncovered and lowered head. He is a reverent witness of the re-birth of the world. An hour ago there was darkness; now there is light. An hour ago the world was dead; now it is gloriously alive. An hour ago there was silence; now there is sound of such exquisite quality as to ravish the soul with delight. As the first beams of sunlight come streaming over the hills, ten thousand birds join in a mighty chorus of welcome to the newborn day and the world is flooded with song; and the [39]whilom sluggard thrills under the spell of the scene and feels himself a part of the world that is vibrant with music. Can it be denied that this man is all the better citizen for his ability to appreciate the wonderfulness of a sunrise?

But while we extol and magnify the quality of appreciation, it is well to note that it cannot be superinduced by any imperial mandate nor does it spring into being at the behest of didacticism. It can be caught but not taught. Indeed, it is worthy of general observation that the choice things which young people receive from the schools, colleges, and normal schools are caught and not taught, however much the teachers may plume themselves upon their ability to impart instruction. Education, at its best, is a process of inoculation. The teacher is an important factor in this process of generating situations that render inoculation far more easy; and we omit one of the most vital things in education when we refer only to the teacher's ability to "impart instruction." The pupil gets certain things in that room, but the teacher does not give them. The teacher's function is to create situations in which the spirit of the pupil will become inoculated with the germs of truth in all its aspects. If he could give the things that the pupils get, then all would share alike in the distribution. If the teacher could impart instruction, he certainly would not fail to lift all his pupils over the seventy-five per cent hurdle.

If instruction or knowledge could be imparted, education would no longer be a spiritual process but rather one of driving the boy into a corner, imparting such instruction as the teacher might decree and keeping on until the point of saturation was reached or the supply of instruction became exhausted, when the trick would [40]be done. The process would be as simple as pouring water from one vessel into another. Sometimes the teacher of literature strives to engender appreciation in a pupil by rhapsodizing over some passage. She reads the passage in a frenzy of simulated enthusiasm, with a quaver in her voice and moisture in her eyes, only to find, at the end, that her patient has fallen asleep. Appreciation cannot be generated in such fashion. The boy cannot light his torch of appreciation at a mere phosphorescent glow. There must be heat behind the light or there can be no ignition. The boy senses the fictitious at once and cannot react to what he knows to be spurious. Only the genuine can win his interest.

Napoleon Bonaparte once said that no one can gaze into the starry sky at night for five minutes and not believe in the existence of God. But to people who lack such appreciation the night sky is devoid of significance. There are teachers who never go forth to revel in the glories of this star-lit masterpiece of creation, because, forsooth, they are too busy grading papers in literature. Such a teacher is not likely to be the cause of a spiritual ignition in her pupils, for she herself lacks the divine fire of appreciation. If she only possessed this quality no words would be needed to reveal its presence to the boy; he would know it even as the homing-pigeon knows its course. When the spirits of teacher and pupils become merged as they must become in all true teaching, the boy will find himself in possession of this spiritual quality. He knows that he has it, the teacher knows that he has it, and his associates know that he has it, and one and all know that it is well worth having.

It is related of Keats that in reading Spenser he [41]was thrown into a paroxysm of delight over the expression "sea-shouldering whales." The churl would not give a second thought to the phrase, or, indeed, a first one; but the man of appreciation finds in it a source of pleasure. Arlo Bates speaks with enthusiasm of the word "highly" as used in the Gettysburg Speech, and the teacher's work reaches a high point of excellence when it has given to the pupil such a feeling of appreciation as enables him to discover and rejoice in such niceties of literary expression. It widens the horizon of life to him and gives him a deeper and closer sympathy with every form and manifestation of life. Every phase of life makes an appeal to him, from bird on the wing to rushing avalanche; from the blade of grass to the boundless plains; from the prattle of the child to the word miracles of Shakespeare; from the stable of Bethany to the Mount of Transfiguration.

Geography lends itself admirably to the development of appreciation if it is well taught. Indeed, to develop appreciation seems to be the prime function of geography, and the marvel is that it has not been so proclaimed. In this field geography finds a clear justification, and the superintendent who sets forth appreciation as the end and geography as the means is certain to win the plaudits of many people who have long been wondering why there is so much geography in the present course of study. Certainly no appreciation can develop from the question and answer method, for no spiritual quality can thrive under such deadening conditions. If the questions emanated from the pupils, the situation would be improved, but such is rarely the case. Teaching is, in reality, a transfusion of spirit, and when this flow of spirit from teacher to pupil is unimpeded teaching is at high tide. When the subject is [42]artfully and artistically developed the effect upon the child is much the same as that of unrolling a great and beautiful picture. The Mississippi River can be taught as a great drama, from its rise in Lake Itasca to its triumphal entry into the Gulf. As it takes its way southward pine forests wave their salutes, then wheat fields, then corn fields, and, later, cotton fields. Then its tributaries may be seen coming upon the stage to help swell the mighty sweep of progress toward the sea. When geography is taught as a drama, appreciation is inevitable.

The resourceful teacher can find a thousand dramas in the books on geography if she knows how to interpret the pages of the books, and with these inspiring dramas she can lift her pupils to the very pinnacle of appreciation. Such tales are as fascinating as fairy stories and have the added charm of being true to the teachings of science. A raindrop seems a common thing, but cast in dramatic form it becomes of rare charm. It slides from the roof of the house and finds its way into the tiny rivulet, then into the brook, then into the river and thus finally reaches the sea. By the process of evaporation, it is transformed into vapor and is carried over the land by currents of air. As it comes into contact with colder currents, condensation ensues and then precipitation, and our raindrop descends to earth once more. Sinking into the soil at the foot of the tree it is taken up into the tree by capillary attraction, out through the branches and then into the fruit. Then comes the sunshine to ripen the fruit, and finally this fruit is harvested and borne to the market, whence it reaches the home. Here it is served at the breakfast table and the curtain of our drama goes down with our raindrop as orange-juice on the lip of the little girl.

[43]When we come to realize, in our enlarged vision, the possibilities of geography in fostering the quality of appreciation, our teaching of the subject will be changed and vitalized, our textbooks will be written from a different angle, and our pupils will receive a much larger return upon their investment of time and effort. The study of geography will be far less like the conning of a gazetteer or a city directory and more like a fascinating story. In our astronomical geography we shall make many a pleasing excursion into the far spaces and win stimulating glimpses into the infinities. In our physical geography we shall read marvelous stories that outrival the romances of Dumas and Hugo. And geography as a whole will reveal herself as the cherishing mother of us all, providing us with food, and drink, and shelter, and raiment, giving us poetry, and song, and story, and weaving golden fancies for the fabric of our daily dreams.

And when, at length, through the agency of geography and the other means at hand, our young people have achieved the endowment of appreciation, life will be for them a fuller and richer experience and they will be better fitted to play their parts as intelligent, cultivated men and women. The gateways will stand wide open through which they can enter into the palace of life to revel in all its beauteous splendor. They will receive a welcome into the friendship of the worthy good and great of all ages. When they have gained an appreciation of the real meaning of literature, children who have become immortal will cluster about them and nestle close in their thoughts and affections,—Tiny Tim, Little Jo, Little Nell, Little Boy Blue, and Eppie. A visitor in Turner's studio once said to the artist, "Really, Mr. Turner, I can't see in nature the colors [44]you portray on canvas." Whereupon the artist replied, "Don't you wish you could?" When our pupils gain the ability to read and enjoy the message of the artist they will be able to hold communion with Raphael, Michael Angelo, Murillo, Rembrandt, Rosa Bonheur, Titian, Corot, Andrea del Sarto, Correggio, Fra Angelico, and Ghiberti. In the realms of poetry they will be able to hold agreeable converse with Shelley, Keats, Southey, Mrs. Browning, Milton, Victor Hugo, Hawthorne, Poe, and Shakespeare. And when the great procession of artists, poets, scientists, historians, dramatists, statesmen, and philanthropists file by to greet their gaze, entranced they will be able to applaud.

[45]

Chapter Six

Aspiration

Return to Table of Contents

Browning says, "'Tis not what man Does which exalts him, but what man Would do." The boy who has acquired the habit of wishing ardently in right directions is well on the way toward becoming educated. For earnest wishing precedes and conditions every achievement that is worthy the name. The man who does not wish does not achieve, and the man who does wish with persistency and consistency does not fail of achievement. Had Columbus not wished with consuming ardor to circumnavigate the globe, he would never have encountered America. The Atlantic cable figured in the dreams and wishes of Cyrus W. Field long before even the preliminaries became realities. The wish evermore precedes the blueprint. It required forty-two years for Ghiberti to translate his dream into the reality that we know as the bronze doors of the Baptistry. But had there been no dreams there had been no bronze doors, and the world of art would have been the poorer. Every tunnel that pierces a mountain; every bridge that spans a river; every building whose turrets pierce the sky; every invention that lifts a burden from the shoulders of humanity; every reform that gilds the world with the glow of hope, was preceded by a wish whose gossamer strands were woven in a human brain. The Red Cross of today is but a dream of Henri Dunant realized and grown large.

The student who scans the records of historical achievements and of the triumphs of art, music, science, literature, and philanthropy must realize that ardent [46]wishing is the condition precedent to further extension in any of these lines, and he must be aware, too, that the ranks of wishers must be recruited from among the children of our schools. The yearning to achieve is the urge of the divine part of each one of us, and it naturally follows that whoever does not have this yearning has been reduced to the plane of abnormality in that the divine part of him has been subordinated, submerged, stifled. Every fervent wish is a prayer that emanates from this divine part of us, and, in all reverence, it may be said that we help to answer our own prayers. When we wish ardently we work earnestly to cause our dreams to come true. We are told that every wish comes true if we only wish hard enough, and this statement finds abundant confirmation in the experiences of those who have achieved.

The child's wishes have their origin and abode in his native interests and when we have determined what his wishes are, we have in hand the clue that will lead us to the inmost shrine of his native tendencies. This, as has been so frequently said, is the point of attack for all our teaching, this the particular point that is most sensitive to educational inoculation. If we find that the boy is eager to have a wireless outfit and is working with supreme intensity to crystallize his wish into tangible and workable form, quite heedless of clock hours, it were unkind to the point of cruelty and altogether unpedagogical to force him away from this congenial task into some other work that he will do only in a heartless and perfunctory way. If we yearn to have him study Latin, we shall do well to carry the wireless outfit over into the Latin field, for the boy will surely follow wherever this outfit leads. But if we destroy the wireless apparatus, in the hope that we [47]shall thus stimulate his interest in Latin, the scar that we shall leave upon his spirit will rise in judgment against us to the end of life. The Latin may be desirable and necessary for the boy, but the wireless comes first in his wishes and we must go to the Latin by way of the wireless.

It is the high privilege of the teacher to make and keep her pupils hungry, to stimulate in them an incessant ardent longing and yearning. This is her chief function. If she does this she will have great occasion to congratulate herself upon her own progress as well as theirs. If they are kept hungry, the sources of supply will not be able to elude them, for children have great facility and resourcefulness in the art of foraging. They readily discover the lurking places of the substantials as well as of the tid-bits and the sweets. They easily scent the trail of the food for which their spiritual or bodily hunger calls. The boy who yearns for the wireless need not be told where he may find screws, bolts, and hammer. The girl who yearns to paint will somehow achieve pigments, brushes, palette, and teachers. Appetite is the principal thing; the rest comes easy. The hungry child lays the whole world under tribute and cheerfully appropriates whatever fits into his wishes. If his neighbor a mile distant has a book for which he feels a craving, the two-mile walk in quest of that book is invested with supreme charm, no matter what the weather. The apple may be hanging on the topmost bough, but the boy who is apple-hungry recks not of height nor of the labyrinth of hostile branches. He gets the apple. As some one has said, "The soul reaches out for the cloak that fits it."

There is nothing more pathetic in the whole realm [48]of school procedure than the frantic efforts of some teachers to feed their pupils instead of striving to create spiritual hunger. They require pupils to "take" so many problems, con so many words of spelling, turn so many pages of a book on history, and then have them try to repeat in an agony of effort words from a book that they neither understand nor feel an interest in. The teacher would feed them whether they have any craving for food or not. Such teachers seem to be immune to the teachings of psychology and pedagogy; they continue to travel the way their grandparents trod, spurning the practices of Pestalozzi, Froebel, and Francis Parker. They seem not to know that their pupils are predatory beings who are quite capable of ransacking creation to get the food for which they feel a craving. Not appreciating the nature of their pupils, they continue the process of feeding and stuffing them and thus fall into the fatal blunder of mistaking distention for education.

Ruth McEnery Stuart has set out this whole matter most lucidly and cogently in her volume entitled *Sonny*. In this story the boy had four teachers who took no account of his aspirations and natural tendencies, but insisted upon feeding him traditional food by traditional methods. To them it mattered not that he was unlike other boys. What was suitable for them must be equally suitable for him. The story goes that a certain school-master was expounding the passage "Be ye pure in heart." Turning to the boys he exclaimed, "Are you pure in heart? If you're not, I'll flog you till you are." So with Sonny's four teachers. If he had no appetite for their kind of food, they'd feed it to him till he had. But when the appetite failed to come as the result of their much feeding, they [49]banished him to outer darkness with epithets expressive of their disappointment and disgust. They washed their hands of him and were glad to be rid of him.

His next teacher, however, was different. She sensed his unlikeness to other boys and knew, instinctively, that his case demanded and deserved special treatment. She consulted his aspirations and appraised his native tendencies. In doing so, she discovered an embryo naturalist and thus became aware of the task to which she must address herself. So she spread her nets for all living and creeping things, for the beasts of the forest, the birds of the air, for plants, and flowers, and stones,—in short, for all the works of nature. In name she was his teacher, but in reality she was his pupil, and his other four teachers might have become members of the class with rich profit to themselves. In his examination for graduation the boy utterly confounded and routed the members of the examining committee by the profundity and breadth of his knowledge and they were glad to check his onslaught upon the ramparts of their ignorance by awarding him a diploma.

It devolves upon the superintendent and teachers, therefore, to determine what studies already in the schools or what others that may be introduced will best serve the purpose of fostering aspiration. They cannot deny that this quality is an essential element in the spiritual composition of every well-conditioned child as well as of every rightly constituted man and woman. For aspiration means life, and the lack of aspiration means death. The man who lacks aspiration is static, dormant, lifeless, inert; the man who has aspiration is dynamic, forceful, potent, regnant. Aspiration is the animating power that gives wings to the forces of life. It is the motive power that induces the [50]currents of life. The man who has aspiration yearns to climb to higher levels, to make excursions into the realms that lie beyond his present horizon, and to traverse the region that lies between what he now is and what he may become. It is the dove that goes forth from the ark to make discovery of the new lands that beckon.

In a former book the author tried to set forth the influence of the poet in generating aspiration, and in this attempt used the following words: "When he would teach men to aspire he writes *Excelsior* and so causes them to know that only he who aspires really lives. They see the groundling, the boor, the drudge, and the clown content to dwell in the valley amid the loaves and fishes of animal desires, while the man who aspires is struggling toward the heights whence he may gain an outlook upon the glories that are, know the throb and thrill of new life, and experience the swing and sweep of spiritual impulses. He makes them to know that the man who aspires recks not of cold, of storm, or of snow, if only he may reach the summit and lave his soul in the glory that crowns the marriage of earth and sky. They feel that the aspirant is but yielding obedience to the behests of his better self to scale the heights where sublimity dwells."

It were useless for teachers to pooh-pooh this matter as visionary and inconsequential or to disregard aspiration as a vital factor in the scheme of education. This quality is fundamental and may not, therefore, be either disregarded or slurred. Fundamental qualities must engage the thoughtful attention of all true educators, for these fundamentals must constitute the ground-work of every reform in our school procedure. There can be life without arithmetic, but there can be no [51]real life without aspiration. It points to higher and fairer levels of life and impels its possessor onward and upward. This needs to be fully recognized by the schools that would perform their high functions worthily, and no teacher can with impunity evade this responsibility. Somehow, we must contrive to instill the quality of aspiration into the lives of our pupils if we would acquit ourselves of this obligation. To do less than this is to convict ourselves of stolidity or impotence.

Chief among the agencies that may be made to contribute generously in this high enterprise is history, or more specifically, biography, which is quintessential history. A boy proceeds upon the assumption that what has been done may be done again and, possibly, done even better. When he reads of the beneficent achievements of Edison he becomes fired with zeal to equal if not surpass these achievements. Obstacles do not daunt the boy who aspires. Everything becomes possible in the light and heat of his zeal. Since Edison did it, he can do it, and no amount of discouragement can dissuade him from his lofty purpose. He sets his goal high and marches toward it with dauntless courage. If a wireless outfit is his goal, bells may ring and clocks may strike, but he hears or heeds them not.

To be effective the teaching of history must be far more than the mere droning over the pages of a book. It must be so vital that it will set the currents of life in motion. In his illuminating report upon the schools of Denmark, Mr. Edwin G. Cooley quotes Bogtrup on the teaching of history as follows: "History does not mean books and maps; it is not to be divided into lessons and gone through with a pointer like any other paltry school subject. History lies before our eyes like a [52]mighty and turbulent ocean, into which the ages run like rivers. Its rushing waves bring to our listening ears the sound of a thousand voices from the olden time. With our pupils we stand on the edge of a cliff and gaze over this great sea; we strive to open their eyes to its power and beauty; we point out the laws of the rise and fall of the waves, and of the strong under-currents. We strive by poetic speech to open their ears to the voices of the sea which in our very blood run through the veins from generation to generation, and, humming and singing, echo in our innermost being."

Such teaching of history as is here portrayed will never fall upon dull ears or unresponsive spirits. It will thrill the youth with a consuming desire to be up and doing. He will ignite at touch of the living fire. His soul will become incandescent and the glow will warm him into noble action. He yearns to emulate the triumphs of those who have preceded him on the stage of endeavor. If he reads "The Message to Garcia" he feels himself pulsating with the zeal to do deeds of valor and heroism. Whether the records deal with Clara Barton, Nathan Hale, Frances Willard, Mrs. Stowe, Columbus, Lincoln, William the Silent, Erasmus, or Raphael, if these people are present as vital entities the young people will thrill under the spell of the entrancing stories. Then will history and biography come into their own as means to a great end, and then will aspiration take its rightful place as one of the large goals in the scheme of education. As Browning says, "A man's reach should exceed his grasp, or what's a heaven for?" and again:

What I aspired to be

And was not, comforts me.

[53]

Chapter Seven

Initiative

Return to Table of Contents

No one who gives the matter thoughtful consideration will ever deprecate or disparage the possession of the virtue of obedience; but, on the other hand, no such thoughtful person will attempt to deny that this virtue, desirable as it is, may be fostered and emphasized to such a degree that its possessor will become a mere automaton. And this is bad; indeed, very bad. We extol obedience, to be sure, but not the sort of blind, unthinking obedience that will reduce its possessor to the status of the mechanical toy which needs only to be wound up and set going. The factory superintendent is glad to have men about him who are able to work efficiently from blueprints; but he is glad, also, to have men about him who can dispense with blueprints altogether or can make their own. The difference between these two types of operatives spells the difference between leadership and mere blind, automatic following. Were all the workers in the factory mere followers, the work would be stereotyped and the factory would be unable to compete with the other factory, where initiative and leadership obtain.

One psychologist avers that ninety per cent of our education comes through imitation; but, even so, it is quite pertinent to inquire into the remaining ten per cent. Conceding that we adopt our styles of wearing apparel at the behest of society; that we fashion and furnish our homes in conformity to prevailing customs; that we permit press and pulpit to formulate for us our opinions and beliefs; in short, that we are imitators up to the full ninety per cent limit, it still must seem [54]obvious to the close observer that the remaining ten per cent has afforded us a vast number and variety of improvements that tend to make life more agreeable. This ten per cent has substituted the modern harvester for the sickle and cradle with which our ancestors harvested their grain; it has brought us the tractor for the turning of the soil in place of the primitive plow; it has enabled us to use the auto-truck in marketing our products instead of the ox-teams of the olden times; it has brought us the telegraph and telephone with which to send the message of our desires across far spaces; and it has supplied us with conveniences and luxuries that our grandparents could not imagine even in their wildest fancies.

A close scrutiny will convince even the most incredulous that many teachers and schools arc doing their utmost, in actual practice if not in theory, to eliminate the ten per cent margin and render their pupils imitators to the full one hundred per cent limit. We force the children to travel our standard pedagogical tracks and strive to fashion and fix them in our standard pedagogical molds. And woe betide the pupil who jumps the track or shows an inclination to travel a route not of the teacher's choosing! He is haled into court forthwith and enjoined to render a strict accounting for his misdoing; for anything that is either less or more than a strict conformity to type is accounted a defection. We demand absolute obedience to the oracular edicts of the school as a passport to favor. Conformity spells salvation for the child and, in the interests of peace, he yields, albeit grudgingly, to the inevitable.

In world affairs we deem initiative a real asset, but one of the saddest of our mistakes in ordering school [55]activities consists in our fervid attempts to prove that the school is detached from life and something quite apart from the world. We would have our pupils believe that, when they are in school, they are neither in nor of the world. At our commencement exercises we tell the graduates that they are now passing across a threshold out into the world; that they are now entering into the realms of real life; and that on the morrow they will experience the initial impact of practical life. These time-worn expressions pass current, at face value, among enthusiastic relatives and friends, but there are those in the audience who know them to be the veriest cant, with no basis either in logic or in common sense. It is nothing short of foolishness to assert that a young person must attain the age of eighteen years before he enters real life. The child knows that his home is a part of the world and an element in life, that the grocery is another part, the post-office still another part, and so on through an almost endless list. Equally well does he know that the school is a part of life, because it enters into his daily experiences the same as the grocery and the post-office. Full well does he know that he is not outside of life when he is in school, and no amount of sophistry can convince him otherwise. If the school is not an integral part of the world and of life, so much the worse for the school and, by the same token, so much the worse for the teacher. Either the school is a part of the world or else it is neither a real nor a worthy school.

The hours which the child spends in school are quite as much a part of his life as any other portion of the day, no matter what activities the school provides, and we do violence to the facts when we assume or argue [56]otherwise. Here is a place for emphasis. Here is the rock on which many a pedagogical bark has suffered shipwreck. We become so engrossed in the mechanics of our task—grades, tests, examinations, and promotions—that we lose sight of the fact that we are dealing with real life in a situation that is a part of the real world. The best preparation for life is to practice life aright, and this is the real function of the school. If teachers only could or would give full recognition to this simple, open truth, there would soon ensue a wide departure from some of our present mechanized methods. But so long as we cling to the traditional notion that school is detached from real life, so long shall we continue to pursue our merry-go-round methods. If we could fully realize that we are teaching life by the laboratory method, many a vague and misty phase of our work would soon become clarified.

Seeing, then, that the school is a cross-section of life, it follows, naturally, that it embodies the identical elements that constitute life as a whole. We all know, by experience, that life abounds in vicissitudes, discouragements, trials, and obstacles, and the school, being a part of real life, must furnish forth the same elements even if of less magnitude. There are obstacles, to be sure, and there should be. Abraham Lincoln once said, "When you can't remove an obstacle, plow around it." But teachers are prone to remove the obstacles from the pathway of their pupils when they should be training them to surmount these obstacles or, failing that for the time being, to plow around them. It is far easier, however, for the teacher to solve the problem for the boy than to stimulate him to solve it independently. If we would train the boy to leap over hurdles, we must supply the hurdles and [57]not remove them from his path. Still further, we must elevate the hurdles, by easy gradations, if we would increase the boy's powers and prowess.

Professor Edgar James Swift says, "Man expends just energy enough to satisfy the demands of the situation in which he is placed." This statement is big with meaning for all who have a true conception of pedagogy and of life. In this sentence we see the finger-board that points toward high achievements in teaching. If the hurdles are too low, the boy becomes flaccid, flabby, sluggish, and lethargic. The hurdles should be just high enough to engage his full strength, physical, mental, and moral. They should ever be a challenge to his best efforts. But they should never be so high that they will invite discouragement, disaster, and failure. The teacher should guard against elevating hurdles as an exhibition of her own reach. The gymnasium is not a stage for exhibitions. On the contrary, it is a place for graduated, cumulative training.

Our inclination is to make life easy and agreeable to our pupils rather than real. To this end we help them over the difficulties, answer questions which they do not ask, and supply them with crutches when we should be training them to walk without artificial aids. The passing mark rather than real training seems to be made the goal of our endeavors even if we enfeeble the child by so doing. We seem to measure our success by the number of promotions and not by the quality of the training we give. We seem to be content to produce weaklings if only we can push them through the gateway of promotion. It matters not that they are unable to find their way alone through the mazes of life; let them acquire that ability later, after they [58]have passed beyond our control. Again quoting from Professor Swift, "Following a leader, even though that leader be the teacher, tends to take from children whatever latent ability for initiative they may have."

There is a story of an indulgent mother who was quite eager that her boy should have a pleasant birthday and so asked him what he would most like to do. The answer came in a flash: "Thank you, Mother, I should most like just to be let alone." This answer leads us at once to the inner sanctuary of childhood. Children yearn to be let alone and must grow restive under the incessant attentions of their elders. In school there is ever such a continuous fusillade of questions and answers, assigning of lessons, recitations, corrections, explanations, and promulgations, rules and restrictions that the children have no time for growing inside. They are not left to their own devices but are pulled and pushed about, and managed, and coddled or coerced all day long, so that there is neither time nor scope for the exercise and development of initiative. The teacher, at times, seems to think of the school as a mammoth syringe with which she is called upon to pump information into her bored but passive pupils.

Silence is the element in which initiative thrives, but our school programs rarely provide any periods of silence. They assume that to be effective a school must be a place of bustle, and hurry, and excitement, not to mention entertainment. Sometimes the child is intent upon explorations among the infinities when the teacher summons him back to earth to cross a *t* or dot an *i*. The teacher who would implant a thought-germ in the minds of her pupils and then allow fifteen minutes of silence for the process of germination, should be ranked as an excellent teacher. When the child [59]is thinking out things for himself the process is favorable to initiative; but when the teacher directs his every movement, thought, and impulse, she is repressing the very quality that makes for initiative and ultimate leadership. When the boy would do some things on his own, the teacher is striving to force him to travel in her groove.

Henderson well says: "We do not invariably cultivate initiative by letting children alone, but in nine cases out of ten it is a highly effective method. In our honest desire for their betterment, the temptation is always to jump in and to do for them, when we would much better keep hands off, and allow them, under favorable conditions, to do for themselves. They may do something which, from an objective point of view, is much less excellent than our own well-considered plan. But education is not an objective process. It is subjective and was wrapped up in the funny blundering little enterprise of the child, rather than in our own intrusive one." The crude product of the boy's work in manual training is far better for him and for the whole process of education than the finished product of the teacher's skill which sometimes passes for the boy's own work. Some manual training teachers have many a sin charged to their account in this line that stands in dire need of forgiveness.

There are many worthy enterprises through which initiative may be fostered. Prominent among these are some of the home and school projects that are in vogue. These projects, when wisely selected with reference to the child's powers and inclination, give scope for the exercise of ingenuity, resourcefulness, perseverance, and unhampered thinking and acting. Besides, some of the by-products are of value, notably self-reliance [60]and self-respect. A child yearns to play a thinking part in the drama of life and not the part of a marionette or jumping-jack that moves only when someone pulls the string. He yearns to be an entity and not a mere echo. Paternalism, in our school work, does not make for self-reliance, and, therefore, is to be deplored. There is small hope for the child without initiative, who is helped over every slightest obstacle, and who acquires the habit of calling for help whenever he encounters a difficulty.

Here we have ample scope for the problem element in teaching and we are recreant to our opportunities and do violence to child-nature if we fail to utilize this method. We are much given to the analytic in our teaching, whereas the pupil enjoys the synthetic. He yearns to make things. Constructing problems in arithmetic, or history, or physics makes a special appeal to him and we do violence to his natural bent if we fail to accord him the opportunity. We can send him in quest of dramatic situations in the poem, or derivatives in his reading lesson, set him thinking of the construction of farm buildings or machinery, or lead him to seek the causes that led up to events in history. In brief, we can appeal to his curiosity and intelligence and so engage the intensest interest of the whole boy.

A school girl assumed the task of looking after all the repairs in the way of plumbing in the home and, certainly, was none the worse for the experience. She is now a dentist and has achieved distinction both at home and abroad in her chosen profession. She gained the habit of meeting difficult situations without abatement of dignity or refinement. The school, at its best, is a favorable situation for self-education and the wise teacher will see to it that it does not decline from [61]this high plane. Only so will its products be young men and women who need no leading strings, who can find their way about through the labyrinth of life and not be abashed. They are the ones to whom we must look for leadership in all the enterprises of life, for they have learned how to initiate work and carry it through to success. That school will win distinction which makes initiative one of its big goals and is diligent in causing the activities of the pupils to reach upward toward the achievement of this end.

We may well conclude with a quotation from Dr. Henry van Dyke: "The mere pursuit of knowledge is not necessarily an emancipating thing. There is a kind of reading which is as passive as massage. There is a kind of study which fattens the mind for examination like a prize pig for a county fair. No doubt the beginning of instruction must lie chiefly in exercises of perception and memory. But at a certain point the reason and the judgment must be awakened and brought into voluntary play. As a teacher I would far rather have a pupil give an incorrect answer in a way which showed that he had really been thinking about the subject, than a literally correct answer in a way which showed that he had merely swallowed what I had told him, and regurgitated it on the examination paper."

[62]

Chapter Eight

Imagination

Return to Table of Contents

In his very stimulating book, *Learning and Doing,* Professor Swift quotes from a business man as follows: "Modern business no longer waits for men to qualify after promotion. Through anticipation and prior preparation every growing man must be largely ready for his new job when it comes to him. I find very few individuals make any effort to think out better ways of doing things. They do not anticipate needs, do not keep themselves fresh at the growing point. If ever they had any imagination they seem to have lost it, and imagination is needed in a growing business, for it is through the imagination that one anticipates future changes and so prepares for them before they come. Accordingly, as a general proposition, the selection of a man for a vacancy within the organization is more or less a matter of guesswork. Now and then an ambitious, wide-awake young man works into the organization and in a very short time is spotted by various department managers for future promotion, but the number of such individuals is discouragingly small. The difficulty with which we are always confronted is that our business grows faster than do those within it. The men do not keep up with our changes. The business grows away from them, and quite reluctantly the management is frequently compelled to go outside for necessary material. We need, at the present time, four or five subordinate chiefs in various parts of the factory and I can fill none of the positions satisfactorily from material in hand."

This business man, unconsciously perhaps, puts his [63]finger upon one of the weak places in our school procedure. He convicts us of stifling and repressing the imagination of our pupils. For it is a matter of common knowledge that every normal child is endowed with a vivid imagination when he enters school. No one will challenge this statement who has entered into the heart of childhood through the gateway of play. He has seen a rag doll invested with all the graces of a princess; he has seen empty spools take on all the attributes of the railway train; and he has seen the child's world peopled with entities of which the unimaginative person cannot know. Children revel in the lore of fairyland, and in this realm nothing seems impossible to them. Their toys are the material which their imagination uses in building new and delightful worlds for them. If this imagination is unimpaired when they become grown-ups, these toys are called ideals, and these ideals are the material that enter into the lives of poets, artists, inventors, scientists, orators, statesmen, and reformers. If the child lacks this quality at the end of his school life, the school must be held responsible, at least in part, and so must face the charge of doing him an irreparable injury. It were better by far for the child to lose a leg or an arm somewhere along the school way than to lose his imagination. Better abandon the school altogether if it tends to quench the divine fire of imagination. Better still, devise some plan of so reconstructing the work of the school that we shall forever forestall the possibility of producing a generation of spiritual cripples.

The business man already quoted gives to the schools their cue. He shows the need of imagination in practical affairs and, by implication, shows that the school has been recreant to its opportunities in the way of [64]stimulating this requisite quality. We must be quite aware that the men and women who have done things as well as those who are doing things have had or have imagination. Otherwise no achievements would be set down to their credit. It is the very acme of unwisdom to expect our pupils to accomplish things and then take from them the tools of their craft. Imagination is an indispensable tool, and the teacher assumes a grave responsibility who either destroys or blunts it. Unless the school promotes imagination it is not really a school, seeing that it omits from its plans and practices this basic quality. Too much emphasis cannot be laid upon this patent truth, nor can we deplore too earnestly the tendency of many teachers to strangle imagination.

We all recognize C. Hanford Henderson as one of our most fertile and sane writers on educational themes and we cannot do better just here than to quote, even at some length, from his facile pen: "To say of man or woman that they have no imagination is to convict them of many actual and potential sins. Such a defect means obtuseness in manners and morals, sterility in arts and science, blundering in the general conduct of life. Children are often accused of having too much imagination, but in reality that is hardly possible.

The imagination may run riot, and, growing by what it feeds upon, come dangerously near to untruthfulness,—the store of facts may have been too small. But the remedy is not to cripple or kill the imagination; it is rather to provide the needed equipment of facts and to train the imagination to work within the limits of truth and probability. The unimaginative man is exceedingly dull company. From the moment he opens his eyes in the morning until he closes [65]them at night, he is prone to the sins of both omission and commission. No matter how good his intentions, he constantly offends. No matter how great his industry, he fails to attain. One can trace many immoralities, from slight breaches of manners to grave criminal offenses, to a simple lack of imagination. The offender failed to see,—he was, to all intents and purposes, blind. At its best, imagination is insight. It is the direct source of most of our social amenities, of toleration, charity, consideration,—in a word, of all those social virtues which distinguish the child of light." Another fertile writer says: "Many a child has been driven with a soul-wound into corroding silence by parents who thought they were punishing falsehood when they were in reality repressing the imagination—the faculty which master-artists denote as the first and loveliest possession of the creative mind."

Some of our boys will be farmers but, if they lack imagination, they will be dull fellows, at the very best, and, relatively speaking, not far above the horse that draws the plow. The girls will be able to talk, but if they lack imagination they can never become conversationalists. The person who has imagination can cause the facts of the multiplication table to scintillate and glow. The person who lacks imagination is unable to invest with interest and charm even the mountain, the river, the landscape, or the poem. The gossip, the scandal-monger, or the coarse jester proves his lack of imagination and his consequent inability to hold his own in real conversation. We hope, of course, that some of our pupils may become inventors, but this will be impossible unless they possess imagination. A sociologist states the case in this fashion: "Wealth, the transient, is material; achievement, the [66]enduring, is immaterial. The products of achievement are not material things at all. They are not ends, but means. They are methods, ways, devices, arts, systems, institutions.

In a word, they are *inventions*." In short, to say that one is an inventor is but another way of saying that he has imagination.

It is one thing to know facts but quite another thing to know the significance of facts. And imagination is the alembic that discovers the significance of the facts. A thousand men of England knew the facts touching the life and education of the children of that country, but the facts remained mere facts until the imagination of Dickens interpreted them and thus emancipated childhood from the thralldom of ignorance and cruelty. A thousand men knew the fact touching the steam that issues from the tea-kettle, but not until Watts discovered the significance of the fact did the tea-kettle become the precursor of the steam-engine that has transformed civilization. It required the imagination of Newton to interpret the falling of the apple and to cause this simple, common fact to lead on to the discovery of the great truth of gravitation. Had Galileo lacked imagination, the chandelier might have kept on swinging but the discovery of the rotation of the earth would certainly have been postponed.

In this view of the matter we can see one of the weaknesses of some of the work in our colleges as well as in other schools. The teachers are fertile in arriving at facts, but seem to think their tasks completed with these discoveries and so proclaim the discovery of facts to be education. It matters not that the facts are devoid of significance to their students, they simply proceed to the discovery of more facts. They combine two or more substances in a test-tube and [67]thus produce a new substance. This fact is solemnly inscribed in a notebook and the incident is closed. But the student who has imagination and industry inquires "What then?" and proceeds with investigations on his own initiative that result in a positive boon to humanity. Imagination takes the facts and makes something of them, while the college teacher has disclosed his inability to cope with his own students in fields that only imagination can render productive.

To quote Henderson once again: "In most of our current education, instead of cultivating so valuable a quality, we have stupidly done all that we can to suppress it. We have not sufficiently studied the actual boy before us to find out what he is up to, and what end he has in mind. On the contrary, we proclaim, with curious indifference, some end of our own devising, and with what really amounts to spiritual brutality, we try to drive him towards it. We do this, we irresponsible parents and teachers, because we ourselves lack imagination, and do not see that we are blunting, instead of sharpening, our human tool. Yet we define education in terms of imagination when we say that education is the unfolding and perfecting of the human spirit; or, that education is a setting-up in the heart of the child of a moral and æsthetic revelation of the universe; for the human spirit which we are trying to establish is not a fact, but a gracious possibility of the future."

Happy is the child whose teacher possesses imagination; who can touch the common things of life with the magic wand of her fancy and invest them with supreme charm; who can peer into the future with her pupils and help them translate the bright dreams of today into triumphs in the realms of art, music, science, [68]philosophy, language, and philanthropy; and who builds air-castles of her own and thus has the skill to help the children build theirs. It is not easy, if, indeed, it is possible, for the teacher to quicken imagination in her pupils unless she herself is endowed with this animating quality. Dr. Henry van Dyke puts the case thus: "I care not whether a man is called a tutor, an instructor, or a full professor; nor whether any academic degrees adorn his name; nor how many facts or symbols of facts he has stored away in his brain. If he has these four powers—clear sight, quick imagination, sound reason, strong will—I call him an educated man and fit to be a teacher." And, of a surety, imagination is not the least of these.

To this end every teacher should use every means possible to keep her imagination alive and luxuriant, and never, on any account, permit the exigencies of her task to repress it. The success of her pupils depends upon her, and she should strive against stagnation as she would against death. The passing out, the evaporation of imagination is an insidious process, and when it is gone she is but a barren fig-tree. If her imagination is strong and healthy she cannot have a poor school and her pupils will bless her memory throughout the years. As applying to every grade of school we may well note the words of Van Dyke: "Every true university should make room in its scheme for life out-of-doors. There is much to be said for

John Milton's plan of a school whose pupils should go together each year on long horseback journeys and sailing cruises to see the world. Walter Bagehot said of Shakespeare that he could not walk down a street without knowing what was in it. John Burroughs has a college on a little farm beside the Hudson; and [69]John Muir has a university called Yosemite. If such men cross a field or a thicket they see more than the seven wonders of the world. That is culture. And without it, all scholastic learning is arid, and all the academic degrees known to man are but china oranges hang on a dry tree." And without imagination this type of culture is impossible.

All reforms and, indeed, all progress depend upon imagination. We must be able to picture the world as it ought to be before we can set on foot plans for betterment. It is the high province of the imagination to enter into the feelings and aspirations of others and so be able to lend a hand; to build a better future out of the materials of the present; to soar above the solemnities and conventions of tradition and to smile while soaring; to see the invisible and touch the intangible; and to see the things that are not and call them forth as realities. Seeing that the business man, the fertile-brained essayist, and the gifted poet agree in extolling the potential value of imagination, we have full warrant for according to it an honored place in the curriculum of the school. Too long has it been an incidental minor; it is now high time to advance it to the rank of a major.

[70]

Chapter Nine

Reverence

Return to Table of Contents

At the basis of reverence is respect; and reverence is respect amplified and sublimated. A boy must be either dull or heedless who can look at a bird sailing in the air for five minutes and not become surcharged with curiosity to know how it can do it. His curiosity must lead him to an examination of the wing of a bird, and his scrutiny will reveal it as a marvelous bit of mechanism. The adjustment and overlapping of the feathers will convince him that it presents a wonderful design and a no less wonderful adaptation of means to ends. He sees that when the bird is poised in the air the wing is essentially air-tight and that when the bird elects to ascend or descend the feathers open a free passage for the air. Even a cursory examination of the bird's wing must persuade the boy that, with any skill he might attain, he could never fabricate anything so wonderful. This knowledge must, in the nature of things, beget a feeling of respect, and thereafter, whenever the boy sees a bird, he will experience a resurgence of this feeling.

Some one has said, "Everything is infinitely high that we can't see over," and because the boy comes to know that he cannot duplicate the bird's wing it becomes infinitely high or great to him and so wins his respect. To the boy who has been taught to think seriously, the mode of locomotion of a worm or a snake is likewise a marvel, and he observes it with awe. The boy who treads a worm underfoot gives indisputable evidence that he has never given serious thought to its mode of travel. Had he done so, he would never commit [71]so ruthless an act. The worm would have won his respect by its ability to do a thing at which he himself would certainly fail. He sees the worm scaling the trunk of a tree with the greatest ease, but when he essays the same task he finds it a very difficult matter. So he tips his cap figuratively to the worm and, in boyish fashion, admits that it is the better man of the two. And never again, unless inadvertently, will he crush a worm. Even a snake he will kill only in what he conceives to be self-defense.

An American was making his first trip to Europe. On the way between the Azores and Gibraltar the ship encountered a storm of great violence. For an hour or more the traveler stood on the forward deck, watching the titanic struggle, feeling the ship tremble at each impact of the waves, and hearing the roar that only a storm at sea can produce. Upon returning to his friends he said, "Never again can I speak flippantly of the ocean; never again can I use the expression, 'crossing the pond.' The sea is too vast and too sublime for that." He had achieved reverence. Many a child in school can spell the name of the ocean and give a book definition rather glibly, who, nevertheless, has not the faintest conception of what an ocean really is. The tragedy of the matter is that the teacher gives him a perfect mark for his parrot-like definition and spelling and leaves him in crass ignorance of the reality. The boy deals only with the husk and misses the kernel. When he can spell and define, the work has only just begun, and not until the teacher has contrived to have him emotionalize the ocean will he enter into the heart of its greatness, and power, and utility in promoting life, and so come to experience a feeling of respect for it. When it [72]has won his respect he can read Victor Hugo's matchless description of the sea with understanding, measurable appreciation, and, certainly, a thrill of delight.

It is rare fun for children, and even for grown-ups, to locate the constellations, planets, and stars. Of course, the North Star is everybody's favorite because it is so steady, so reliable, so dependable. We know just where to find it, and it never disappoints us. Two boys who once were crossing from New York to Naples found great delight in a star in the Southern sky that retained its relative position throughout the journey. At the conclusion of dinner in the evening the boys were wont to repair to the deck to find their star and receive its greetings. In their passage through the Mediterranean they became curious, wondering how it came about that the star failed to change its relative position in their journey of three thousand miles. When they realized that their star is the apex of a triangle whose base is three thousand miles but whose other legs are so long that the base is infinitesimally short by comparison, their amazement knew no bounds and for the first time in their lives they gained a profound respect for space.

This new concept of space was worth the trip across the ocean to those boys, and the wonder is that space had never before meant anything more or other than a word to be spelled. The school and the home had had boundless opportunities to inculcate in them a sense of space, yet this delightful task was left to a passenger on board the ship. But for his kindly offices those boys might have gone on for years conceiving of space as merely a word of five letters. It would have been easy for parent or teacher to engender in them some appreciation of space by explaining [73]to them that if they were to travel thirty miles a day it would require twenty-two years to reach the moon,—which is, in reality, our next-door neighbor,—and that to reach the sun, at the same rate of travel, would require more than eight thousand years, or the added lifetimes of almost three hundred generations. But they were sent abroad to see the wonders of the Old World with no real conception of space and, therefore, no feeling of respect for it. Before their trip abroad they never could have read the last two verses of the eighth chapter of Romans with any real appreciation.

Still our schools go on their complacent way, teaching words, words, words that are utterly devoid of meaning to the pupils, and, sad to relate, seem to think their mission accomplished. The pupils are required to spell words, define words, write words, and parse words day after day as if these words were lifeless and meaningless blocks of wood to be merely tossed up and down and moved hither and thither. So soon as a word becomes instinct with life and meaning, it kindles the child's interest at its every recurrence and it becomes as truly an entity as a person. It is then endowed with attributes that distinguish it clearly from its fellows and becomes, to the child, a vivid reality in the scheme of life. To our two boys every star that meets their gaze conjures up a host of memories and helps to renew their spiritual experience and widen their horizon. Space is a reality, to them, a mighty reality, and they cannot think of it without a deep sense of respect.

There are people of mature years who have never given to their hands a close examination. Such an examination will disclose the fact that the hand is an instrument of marvelous design. It will be seen that [74]the fingers all differ in length but, when they grasp an orange or a ball, it will be noted that they are conterminous—that the ends form a straight line. This gives them added purchase and far greater power of resistance. Were they of equal length the pressure upon the ball would be distributed and it could be wrested from the grasp far more readily. No mechanical contrivance has ever been designed that is comparable to the hand in flexibility, deftness, adaptability, or power of prehension. It can pick up a needle or a cannon-ball at will. Its touch is as light as a feather or as stark as a catapult. It can be as gentle as mercy or as harsh as battle. It can soothe to repose or rouse to fury. It can express itself in the gentle zephyr or in the devastating whirlwind. Its versatility is altogether worthy of notice, and we may well hold the lesson in history in abeyance, for the nonce, while we inculcate due respect for the hand. For no one can contemplate his hand for five minutes and not gain for it a feeling of profound respect.

What is true of the hand is true of the whole human body. This is the very acme of created things; this is God's masterpiece. How any one can fail to respect such a wonderful piece of work is beyond explanation. The process of walking or of breathing must hold the thoughtful person enthralled and enchanted. But, strange as it may seem, there are those who seem not to realize in what a marvelous abode their spirits have their home. Such scant respect do they have for their bodies that they defile them and treat them with shameless ignominy. They saturate them with poisons and vulgarize them with unseemly practices. They seem to regard them as mere property to be used or abused at pleasure and not temples to be honored. The man [75]who does not respect his own body can feel no respect or reverence for its Creator nor for the soul that dwells within it. Such a man lacks self-respect and self-respect is the fertile soil in which many virtues flourish. The teaching of physiology that fails to generate a feeling of deep respect for the human body is not the sort of teaching that should obtain in our schools.

Again, a person who is possessed of fine sensibilities sees in the apple tree in full bloom a creation of transcendant beauty and charm. The poet cannot describe it, nor can the artist reproduce it. It is both a mystery and a miracle. Into this miracle nature has poured her lavish treasures of fertility, of rain, of sunshine, and of zephyrs, and from it at the zenith of its beauty the full-throated robin pours forth his heart in melodious greeting. It may be well to dismiss the school to see the circus parade, but even more fitting is it to dismiss the school to see this burst of splendor. In its glorious presence silence is the only language that is befitting. In such a presence sound is discord, for such enchantment as it begets cannot be made articulate. Its influence steals into the senses and lifts the spirit up. To defile or despoil such beauty would be to desecrate a shrine. But the sordid man sees in this symphony of color nothing else than a promise of fruit. His response is wholly physical, not spiritual at all. His spiritual sense seems atrophied and he can do nothing but estimate the bushels of fruit. He feels no respect for the beauty before him and it is evident that somewhere along the line his spiritual education was neglected. He excites our sympathy and our hope that his children may not share his fate.

In the way of illustrating this quality of respect, [76]we reach the climax in the thirty-eighth chapter of the Book of Job and following. The dramatic element of literature here reaches its zenith. God is the speaker, the stricken, outcast Job is the sole auditor, and the stage is a whirlwind. It is related of the late Professor Hodge that, on one occasion when he was about to perform an experiment in his laboratory, he said to some students who stood near, "Gentlemen, please remove your hats; I am about to ask God a question." But here in this chapter we have a still more sublime situation, for God is here asking questions of the man. And these questions dig deep into the life of the man and show him how puny and impotent is the finite in the presence of the Infinite. In this presence there is neither pomp, nor parade, nor vaunting, nor self-aggrandizement, nor arrogance. Even the printed page cannot but induce respect, devoutness, and profound reverence, for it tells of nature's wonders—the snow-crystals, the rain, the dewdrop, the light, the cloud, the lightning—and reveals to the bewildered sight some apprehension of the Author of them all.

The reader must, by now, have divined the conclusion of the whole matter. Without respect there can be no reverence; and, without reverence, there can be neither education nor civilization that is worth while. Some one has defined reverence as "that exquisite constraint which leads a man to hate all that is unsuitable and sordid and exaggerated and to love all that is excellent and temperate and beautiful." This definition is both comprehensive and inclusive, and the superintendent may well promulgate it in his directions to his teachers. All teaching has to do with Truth and, in the presence of Truth, whether in mathematics, or science, or history, or language, the teacher should feel that he [77]stands in the presence of the Burning Bush and hears the command, "Put off thy shoes from off thy feet, for the place whereon thou standest is holy ground." It seems a thousand pities that even college students rush into the presence of the Burning Bush in hobnailed shoes, shouting forth the college yell as they go.

The man who is reverent disclaims everything that is cheap, or vulgar, or coarse, or unseemly. He is so essentially fine that the gaudy, the bizarre, and the intemperate, in whatever form, grate upon his sensibilities. He respects himself too much to be lacking in respect to others. He instinctively shrinks away from ugly vulgarization as from a pestilence. He is kindly, charitable, sympathetic, and sincere. Exaggeration, insinuation, and caricature are altogether foreign to his spirit. In his society we feel inspired and ennobled. His very presence is a tonic, and his tongue distills only purity. His example is the lodestar of our aspirations, and we fain would be his disciples. We feel him to be something worshipful in that his life constantly beckons to our better selves. To be reverent is to be liberally educated, while to be irreverent is to dwell in darkness and ignorance. To be reverent is to live on the heights, where the air is pure and tonic and where the sunlight is free from taint. To be reverent is to acknowledge our indebtedness to all those who, in art, in science, in literature, in music, or in philanthropy, have caused the waters of life to gush forth in clear abundance. To be reverent is to stand uncovered in the presence of Life and to experience the thrill of the spiritual impulses that only an appreciation of life can generate. If this is reverence, then the school honors itself by giving this quality a place of honor.

[78]

Chapter Ten

Sense of Responsibility

Return to Table of Contents

Every one who has had to do with Harvey's Grammar will readily recall the sentence, "Milo began to lift the ox when he was a calf." Aside from the interest which this sentence aroused as to the antecedent of the pronoun, it also enunciated a bit of philosophy which caused the pupils to wonder about the possibility of such a feat. They were led to consider such examples of physical strength as Samson, Hercules, and the more modern Sandow and to wonder, perhaps, just what course of training brought these men to their attainment of physical power. It is comparatively easy for adults to realize that such feats as these men accomplished could only come through a long process of training. If a man can lift a given weight on one day, he may be able to lift a slightly heavier weight the next day, and so on until he has achieved distinction by reason of his ability to lift great weights. So it is in this matter of responsibility. It need hardly be said that responsibility is the heaviest burden that men and women are called upon to lift or carry. We need only think of the responsibilities pertaining to the office of the chief ruler of a country in time of war, or of the commanding general of armies, or of the president of large industrial concerns, and so on through the list. Such men bear burdens of responsibility that cannot be estimated in terms of weights or measures. We can easily think of the time when the manager of a great industrial concern was a child in school, but it is not so easy to think of the six-year-old boy performing the functions of this same manager. [79]However, we do know that the future rulers, generals, managers, and superintendents are now sitting at desks in the schools and it behooves all teachers to inquire by what process these pupils may be so trained that in time they will be able to execute these functions.

In some such way we gain a right concept of responsibility. We cannot think of the six-year-old boy as a bank president but, in our thinking, we can watch his progress, in one-day intervals, from his initial experience in school to his assumption of the duties pertaining to the presidency of the bank. In thus tracing his progress there is no strain or stress in our thinking nor does the element of improbability obtrude itself. We think along a straight and level road where no hills arise to obstruct the view. Each succeeding day marks an inch or so of progress toward the goal. But should we set the responsibilities of the bank president over against the powers of the child, the disparity would overwhelm our thinking and our minds would be thrown into confusion. Our thinking is level and easy only when we conceive of strength and responsibility advancing side by side and at the same rate.

It would be an interesting experience to overhear the teacher inquiring of the superintendent how she should proceed in order to inculcate in her pupils a sense of responsibility. We should be acutely alert to catch every word of the superintendent's reply. If he were dealing with such a concrete problem as Milo and the calf, his response would probably be satisfactory; but when such an abstract quality as responsibility is presented to him his reply might be vague and unsatisfactory. His thinking may have had to do with concrete problems so long that an abstract quality presents a real difficulty to his mental operations. Yet the question[80] which the teacher propounds is altogether pertinent and reasonable and, if he fails to give a satisfactory reply, he will certainly decline in her esteem.

The normal child welcomes such a measure of responsibility as falls within the compass of his powers and acquits himself of it in a manner that is worthy of commendation. This open truth encourages the conviction that the superintendent who can give to the teacher a definite plan by which she will be able to develop a sense of responsibility, will commend himself to her favor, if not admiration. They both know full well that if the pupil emerges from the school period lacking this quality he will be a helpless weight upon society and a burden to himself and his family, no matter what his mental attainments. He will be but a child in his ability to cope with situations that confront him and cannot perform the functions of manhood. Though a man in physical stature he will shrink from the ordinary duties that fall to the lot of a man and, like a child, will cling to the hand of his mother for guidance. In all situations he will show himself a spiritual coward.

The problem is easy of statement but by no means so easy of solution. At the age of six the boy takes his place at a desk in the school. Twenty years hence, let us say, he will be a railway engineer. As such he must drive his engine at forty miles an hour through blinding storm, or in inky darkness, or through menacing and stifling tunnels, or over dizzy bridges, or around the curve on the edge of the precipice—and do this with no shadow of fear or hint of trepidation, but always with a keen eye, a cool head, and a steady hand. In his keeping are the lives of many persons, and any wavering or unsteadiness, on his part, may lead to [81]speedy disaster. Somewhere along the way between the ages of six and twenty-six he must gain the ability to assume a heavy responsibility, and it would seem a travesty upon rational education to force him to acquire this ability wholly during the eight years succeeding his school experience. If, at the age of eighteen, he does not exhibit some ability in this respect, the school may justly be charged with dereliction.

Or, twenty years hence, this boy may be a physician. If so, he will find a weeping mother clinging to him and imploring him to save her baby. He will see a strong man broken with sobs and offering him a fortune to save his wife from being engulfed in the dark shadows. His ears will be assailed with delirious ravings that call to him for relief and life. He will be importuned by the grief-crushed child not to let her mother go. He will be called upon to grapple with plague, with pestilence, with death itself. Unless he can give succor, hope departs and darkness enshrouds and blights. He alone can hold disease and death at bay and bid darkness give place to light and cause sorrow to vanish before the smile of joy. He stands alone at the portal to do battle against the demons of devastation and desolation. And, if he fails, the plaints of grief will penetrate the innermost chambers of his soul. He must not fail. So he toils on through the long night watches, disdaining food and rest, that the breaking day may bring in gladness and crown the arts of healing. And the school that does not share in the glory of such achievement misses a noble opportunity.

Again, twenty years hence, the little girl who now sits at her desk, crowned with golden ringlets, will be a wife and mother, and the mistress of a well-conditioned home. She is a composite of Mary and Martha[82] and in her kingdom reigns supreme and benign. In her home there is no hint of "raw haste, half-sister to delay," for long since she acquired the habit of serene mastery. She meets her manifold responsibilities with a smile and sings her way through them all. If clouds arise, she banishes them with the magic of her poise and amiability. She can say with Napoleon, "I do not permit myself to become a victim of circumstances; I make circumstances." Back in the school she learned order, system, method, and acquired the sense of responsibility. At first the teacher's desk was her special care, and by easy gradations the scope of her activities was widened until she came to feel responsible for the appearance of the entire schoolroom. Now in her womanhood she is a delight to her husband, her children, her guests, and her neighbors. Emergencies neither daunt her nor render her timorous, but, serene and masterful, she meets the new situation as a welcome novelty, and, with supreme amiability, accepts it as a friendly challenge to her resourcefulness. She needs not to apologize or explain, for difficulties disappear at her approach because, in the school, responsibility was one of the major goals of her training.

Or, again, two decades hence this child may have attained to a position in the world of affairs where good taste, judgment, perseverance, self-control, graciousness, and tact are accounted assets of value. But these qualities, gained through experience, are as much a part of herself as her hands. A thousand times in the past has the responsibility been laid upon her of making selections touching shapes, colors, materials, or types, till now her judgment is regarded as final. Her self-control has become proverbial, but it is not the miracle that it seems, for it has become grooved [83]into a habit by much experience. She met all these lions in her path at school and vanquished them all, with the aid of the teacher's counsel and encouragement. She can perform heroisms now because she long since contracted the habit of heroisms. And responsibility is most becoming to her now because in the years past she learned how to wear it. She has multiplied her powers and usefulness a hundred-fold by reason of having learned to assume responsibility.

She has learned to lift her eyes and scan the far horizon and not be afraid. With gentle, kindly eyes she can look into the faces of men and women in all lands and not be abashed in their presence. She can soothe the child to rest and prove herself a scourge to evildoers, all within the hour. She knows herself equal to the best, but not above the least. She does not need to pose, for she knows her own power without ever vaunting it. Her simplicity and sincerity are the fragrant bloom of her sense of responsibility both to herself and her kind. She gives of herself and her means as a gracious discharge of obligation to the less fortunate, but never as charity. She feels herself bound up in the interests of humanity and would do her full part in helping to make life more worth while. Her touch has the gift of healing and her tongue distills kindness. Her obligations to the human family are privileges to be esteemed and enjoyed and not bur-dens to be endured and reviled. And she thinks of her superintendent and teachers with gratitude for their part in the process of developing her into what she is, and what she may yet become.

Only such as the defiant, wicked, and rebellious Cain can ask the question, "Am I my brother's keeper?" The man who feels no responsibility for the character [84]and good name of the community of which he is a member is a spiritual outcast and will become a social pariah if he persists in maintaining his attitude of indifference. For, after all, responsibility amounts to a spiritual attitude. If the man feels no responsibility to his community he will begrudge it the taxes he pays, the improvements he is required to make, and will be irked by every advance that makes for civic betterment. To him the church and school will seem excrescences and superfluities, nor would he grieve to see them obliterated. His exodus would prove a distinct boon to the community. He may have a noble physique, good mentality, much knowledge, and large wealth, and yet, with all these things in his favor, he is nevertheless a liability for the single reason that he lacks a sense of responsibility. Could his teachers have foreseen his present attitude no efforts, on their part, would have seemed too great if only they could have forestalled his misfortune. And it is for the teachers to determine whether the boy of today shall become a duplicate of the man here portrayed.

Every man who lives under a democratic form of government has the opportunity before him each day to raise or lower the level of democracy. When the night comes on, if he reflects upon the matter, he must become conscious that he has done either the one or the other. Either democracy is a better thing for humanity because of his day's work and influence, or it is a worse thing. This is a responsibility that he can neither shift nor shirk. It is fastened upon him with or against his will. It rests with him to determine whether he would have every other man and every boy in the land select him as their model and follow his example to the last detail. He alone can decide whether [85]he would have all men indulge in the practices that constitute his daily life, consort with his companions, hold his views on all subjects, read only the books that engage his interest, duplicate his thoughts, aspirations, impulses, and language, and become, each one, his other self. Every boy who now sits in the school must answer these questions for himself sooner or later, nor can he hope to evade them. Happy is that boy, therefore, whose teacher has the foresight and the wisdom to train him into such a sense of responsibility as will enable him to answer them in such a way that the future will bring to him no pang of remorse.

Thomas A. Edison is one of the benefactors of his time. He reached out into space and grasped a substance that is both invisible and intangible, harnessed it with trappings, pushed a button, and the world was illumined. There were years of unremitting toil behind this achievement, years of discouragement bordering on despair, but years in which the light of hope was kept burning. We accept his gift with the very acme of nonchalance and with little or no feeling of gratitude. Perhaps he would not have it otherwise. We do not know. But certain it is that his marvelous achievement has made life more agreeable to millions of people and he must be conscious of this fact. At some time in his life he must have achieved a sense of responsibility to his fellows and this worthy sentiment must have become the guiding principle in all his labors. If some teacher fostered in him this sense of responsibility, she did a piece of work for the world that can never be measured in terms of salary. She did not teach arithmetic, or grammar, or geography. She taught Edison. And one of the big results of her teaching was his attainment of this sense of responsibility which far [86]overtops all the arithmetic and history that he ever learned. The man who carried the message to Garcia is another fitting illustration of this same principle. In executing his commission he overcame difficulties that would have seemed insurmountable to a less intrepid man. He kept his eye on the goal and endured almost unspeakable hardships in pressing forward toward this goal. Somehow and somewhere in his life he had learned the meaning of responsibility and so felt that he must not fail. The world came to know him as a hero because he was a hero at heart and his heroic achievement had its origin in the training that led him to feel a sense of responsibility.

[87]

Chapter Eleven

Loyalty

Return to Table of Contents

When the boy overhears a companion put a slight upon the good name of his mother, he does not deliberate but, like a flash, smites the mouth that defames. He may deliberate afterward, for the mind then has a fact upon which to work, but if he is a worthy son it is not till afterwards. Spiritual impulses are as quick as powder and as direct as a shaft of light. So quick are they that we are prone to disregard them in our contemplation of their results. We see the boy strike and conclude, in a superficial way, that his hand initiated the action, nor take pains to trace this action back to the primal cause in the spiritual impulse. True, both mind and body are called into action, but only as auxiliaries to carry out the behests of the spirit. When the man utters an exclamation of delight at sight of his country's flag in a foreign port, the sound that we hear is but the conclusion or completion of the series of happenings. It is not the initial happening at all. On the instant when his eyes caught sight of the flag something took place inside the man's nature. This spiritual explosion was telegraphed to the mind, the mind, in turn, issued a command to the body, and the sound that was noted was the final result. In a general way, education is the process of training mind and body to obey and execute right commands of the spirit. This definition will justify our characterization of education as a spiritual process.

Seeing, then, that the body is but a helper whose [88]function is to execute the mandates of the spirit, and seeing, too, that education is a process of the spirit, it follows that our concern must be primarily and always with the spirit as major. It is the spirit that reacts, not the mind or the body, and education is, therefore, the process of inducing right reactions of the spirit. The nature of these reactions depends upon the quality of the external stimuli. If we provide the right sort of stimuli the reactions will be right. If, today, the spirit reacts to a beautiful picture, tomorrow, to the tree in bloom, the next day to an alluring landscape, and the next to the glory of a sunrise, in time its reactions to beauty in every form will become habitual. If we can induce reactions, day by day, to beautiful or sublime passages in literature, in due time the spirit will refuse to react to what is shoddy and commonplace. By inducing reactions to increasingly better musical compositions, day after day, we finally inculcate the habit of reacting only to high-grade music, and the lower type makes no appeal. By such a process we shall finally produce an educated, cultivated man or woman, the crowning glory of education.

The measure of our success in this process of education will be the number of reactions we can induce to the right sort of stimuli. In this, we shall have occasion to make many substitutions. The boy who has been reacting to ugliness must be lured away by the substitution of beauty. The beautiful picture will take the place of the bizarre until nothing but such a picture will give pleasure and satisfaction. Indeed, the substitution of beauty for ugliness will, in time, induce a revolt against what is ugly and stimulate the boy to desire to transform the ugly thing into a thing of [89]beauty. Many a home shows the effects of reaction in the school to artistic surroundings. The child reacts to beauty in the school and so yearns for the same sort of stimuli in the home. When the little girl entreats her mother to provide for her such a ribbon as the teacher wears, we see an exemplification of this principle. When only the best in literature, in art, in nature, in music, and in conduct avail to produce reactions, we may well proclaim the one who reacts to these stimuli an educated person. It is well to repeat that these reactions are all spiritual manifestations and that the conduct of mind and body is a resultant.

To casual thinking it may seem a far cry from reactions and external stimuli to loyalty, but not so by any means. The man or woman who has been led to react to the Madonna of the Chair, the Plow Oxen, or the ceiling of the Sistine Chapel will experience a revival and recurrence of the reaction at every sight of the masterpiece, whether the original or a reproduction. That masterpiece has become this person's standard of art and neither argument, nor persuasion, nor sophistry can divorce him from his ideal. The boy's mother is one of his ideals. He believes her to be the best woman alive, and it were a sorry fact if he did not. Hence, when her good qualities are assailed his spirit explodes and commands his right arm to become a battering-ram. The kindness of the mother has caused the boy's spirit to react a thousand times, and his reaction in defending her name from calumny was but another evidence of an acquired spiritual habit.

Hence it is that we find loyalty enmeshed in these elements that pertain to the province of psychology. It must be so, seeing that these elements and loyalty [90]have to do with the spirit, for loyalty is nothing other than a reaction to the same external stimuli that have induced reactions many times before. In setting up loyalty, therefore, as one of the big goals of school endeavor the superintendent has only to make a list of the external stimuli that will induce proper reactions and so groove these reactions into habit. His problem, thus stated, seems altogether simple but, in working out the details, he will find himself facing the entire scheme of education. If he would induce reactions that spell loyalty he must make no mistake in respect of external stimuli, for it must be reiterated that the character of the stimuli conditions the reactions. We may not hope to achieve loyalty unless through the years of training we have provided stimuli of the right sort.

If the sentiment of loyalty concerns itself with the teachings of the Bible and the tenets of the church, we call it religion; if it has to do with one's country and what its flag represents, we call it patriotism; and in many another relation we call it fidelity. Hence it is obvious that loyalty is an inclusive quality and in its ramifications reaches out into every phase of life. This gives us clear warrant for making it one of the prime objectives in a rational, as distinguished from a traditional, scheme of education. The progressive superintendent who is endowed with perspicacity, resourcefulness, altruism, and faith in himself will consult the highest interests of the boys and girls of his school before he relegates the matter to oblivion. To such as he we must look for advance and for the redemption of our schools from their traditional moorings. To such as he we must look for the inoculation of the teachers with such virus as will [91]render them vital, dynamic, and eager to essay any new task that gives promise of a larger and better outlook for their pupils.

In the second chapter of Revelation, tenth verse, we read, "Be thou faithful unto death and I will give thee the crown of life." Now this is quite as true in a psychological sense as it is in a scriptural sense. It is a great pity that we do not read the Bible far more for lessons in pedagogy. However, too many people misread the quoted passage. They interpret the expression "unto death" as if it were "until death." This interpretation would weaken the expression. The martyrs would not recant even when the fires were blazing all about them or when their bodies were lacerated. They were faithful unto death. In his poem *Invictus* Henley says,

> In the fell clutch of circumstance
>
> I have not winced nor cried aloud;
>
> Under the bludgeonings of chance,
>
> My head is bloody but unbowed.

And only so can the spirit hope to achieve emancipation and win out into the clear. This is the crown of life. Michael Angelo represents Joseph of Arimathea standing at the tomb of the Master with head erect and with the mien of faith. He did not understand at all, and yet his faithful heart encouraged him to hope and to hold his head from drooping. He was faithful even in the darkness and on the morning of the Resurrection he received his crown.

When we set up loyalty as one of our major goals we shall become alert to every illustration of it that falls under our gaze. The story of Nathan Hale will become newly alive and will thrill as never before. [92]Over against Nathan Hale we shall set Philip Nolan for the sake of comparison and contrast. Even though our pupils may regard Joan of Arc as a fanatic, her heroism and her fidelity to her convictions will shine forth as a star in the night and her example as illustrating loyalty will be as seed planted in fertile soil. In our quest for exemplars we shall find the pages of history palpitating with life. We may sow dead dragon's teeth, but armed men will spring into being. Thermopylæ will become a new story, while William Tell and Arnold Winkelried will take rank among the demigods. Sidney Carton will become far more than a mere character of fiction, for on his head we shall find a halo, and Horace Mann will become far more than a mere schoolmaster. Historians, poets, novelists, statesmen, and philanthropists will rally about us to reinforce our efforts and to cite to us men and women of all times who shone resplendent by reason of their loyalty.

Our objective being loyalty, we shall omit the lesson in grammar for today in order to induce the spirits of our pupils to react to the story of Jephthah's daughter. For once they have emotionalized it, have really felt its power, this story will become to them a rare possession and will entwine itself in the warp and woof of their lives and form a pattern of exceeding beauty whose colors will not fade. They shall hear the solemn vow of the father to sacrifice unto the Lord the first living creature that meets his gaze after the victory over his enemies. They shall see him returning invested with the glory of the victor. Then the child will be seen running forth to meet him, the first living creature his gaze has fallen upon since the battle. They will note her gladness to see him and [93]to know that he is safe. They will see the dancing of her eyes and hear her rippling, joyous laughter. They will become tense as the father is telling her of his vow. But the climax is reached when they hear her saying, "My father, if thou hast opened thy mouth unto the Lord, do to me according to that which hath proceeded out of thy mouth." And, with bated breath, they see her meeting death with a smile that her father may keep his covenant with the Lord. Ever after this story will mark to them the very zenith of loyalty, and the lesson in grammar can await another day.

Again, instead of the regular reading lesson the school may well substitute the story of David, as given in the eleventh chapter of Chronicles. "Now three of the thirty captains went down to the rock to David, into the cave of Adullam; and the host of the Philistines encamped in the valley of Rephaim. And David was then in the hold, and the Philistines' garrison was then at Bethlehem. And David longed, and said, 'O that one would give me drink of the water of the well of Bethlehem that is at the gate.' And the three brake through the host of the Philistines, and drew water out of the well of Bethlehem, that was by the gate, and took it, and brought it to David; but David would not drink of it, but poured it out to the Lord, and said, 'My God forbid it me, that I should do this thing. Shall I drink the blood of these men that have put their lives in jeopardy? for with the jeopardy of their lives they brought.' Therefore he would not drink it."

Without any semblance of irreverence we may paraphrase this story slightly and have our own General Pershing stand in the place of David asking for water. Then we can see three of his soldiers going across No Man's Land in quest of the water which he craves. [94]When they return, bearing the water to him from the spring in the enemy's territory, we can see him pouring the water upon the ground and refusing to drink it because of the hazard of the enterprise. No fulsome explanation will need to be given to impress upon the pupils the loyalty of the soldiers to their general, nor yet the loyalty of the general to his soldiers. Or again, in the oral English two of the pupils may be asked to tell the stories of Ruth and Esther, and certain it is, if these stories are told effectively, the pupils will thrill with admiration for the loyalty of these two noble characters.

On his way home for vacation a college student was telling his companion on the train of the trip ahead, relating that at such a time he would reach the junction and at a certain hour he would walk into his home just in time for supper; he concluded by paying a tribute to the noble qualities of his mother. This man is now an attorney in a large city and it is inconceivable that he can ever be guilty of apostasy from the ideals and principles to which he reacted in his boyhood in that village home. Whatever temptations may come to him, the mother's face and voice and the memory of her high principles will forbid his yielding and hold him steady and loyal to that mother and her teaching. He must feel that if he should debase himself he would dishonor her, and that he cannot do. He can still hear her voice echoing from the years long gone, and feel the kindly touch of her hand upon his brow. When troubles came, mother knew just what to do and soon the sun was shining again. It was her magic that made the rough places smooth, her voice that exorcised all evil spirits. She it was who drove the lions from his path and made it a place of peace [95]and joy. To be disloyal to her would be to lose his manhood.

Whatever vicissitudes befall, we yearn to return to the old homestead, for there, and there alone, can we experience, in full measure, the reactions that came from our early associations with the old well, the bridge that spans the brook, the trees bending low with their luscious fruit, the grape arbor, the spring that bubbles and laughs as it gives forth its limpid treasure, the fields that are redolent of the harvest season, and the royal meal on the back porch. The man who does not smile in recalling such scenes of his boyhood days is abnormal, disloyal, and an apostate. These are the scenes that anchor the soul and give meaning to civilization. The man who will not fight for the old home, and for the memory of father and mother, will not fight for the flag of his country and is, at heart, an alien. But the man who is loyal to the home of his early years, loyal to the memory of his parents, and loyal to the principles which they implanted in his life, such a man can never be less than loyal to the flag that floats over him, loyal to the land in which he finds his home, and ever loyal to the best and highest interests of that land. Never, because of him, will the colors of the flag lose their luster or the stars grow dim. He will be faithful even unto death, because loyalty throbs in his every pulsation, is proclaimed by his every word, is enmeshed in every drop of his blood and has become a vital part of himself.

[96]

Chapter Twelve

Democracy

Return to Table of Contents

In a recent book H.G. Wells says that education has lost its way. Whether we give assent to this statement or not, it must be admitted that it is a direct challenge to the school, the home, the pulpit, the press, to government, and to society. If education has indeed lost its way, the responsibility rests with these educational agencies. If education has lost its way, these agencies must unite in a benevolent conspiracy to help it find it again. The war has brought these agencies into much closer fellowship and they are now working in greater harmony than ever before. This is due to the fact that they are working to a common end, that they are animated by a common purpose. The war is producing many readjustments and a new scale of values. Many things that were once considered majors are now thought of as minors, and the work of reconstruction has only just begun. Civilization is now in the throes of a re-birth and people are awakening from their complacency and thinking out toward the big things of life. They are lifting their gaze above and beyond party, and creed, and racial ties, and territorial boundaries, and fixing it upon their big common interests. More and more has their thinking been focused upon democracy, until this has become a watchword throughout the world. About this focal point people's thoughts are rallying day by day, and their community of feeling and thinking is leading to community of action.

Primarily, democracy is a spiritual impulse, the quintessence of the Golden Rule. "As a man thinketh [97]in his heart so is he," and this spiritual quality inevitably precedes and conditions democracy in its outward manifestations. Feeling, thinking, willing, doing—these are the stages in the law of life. The Golden Rule in action has its inception in the love of man for his fellow-man. The action is but the visible fruitage of the invisible spiritual impulse. The soldier in the trench, the sailor on the ship, the nurse in the hospital, the worker in the factory, and the official at his desk, all exemplify this principle. The outward manifestations of the inward impulse, democracy, are many and varied, and the demands of the war greatly increased both the number and variety. People essayed tasks that, a few years ago, would have seemed impossible; nor did they demean themselves in so doing. The production and conservation of food has become a national enterprise that has enlisted the active coöperation of men, women, and children of all classes, creeds, and conditions. Rich and poor joined in the work of war gardens, thinking all the while not only of their own larders but quite as much of their friends across the sea. And while they helped win the war, they were winning their own souls, for they were yielding obedience to a spiritual impulse and not a mere animal desire. Thus Americans and the people of other lands, like children at school, are learning the lesson of democracy. Moreover, they are now appalled at the wastage of former years and at the cheapness of many of the things that once held their interest.

In this process of achieving an access of democracy it holds true that "There is no impression without expression." Each reaction of the spirit tends to groove the impression into a habit, and this process has had a thousand exemplifications before our eyes since the [98]opening of the war. People who were only mildly inoculated with the democratic spirit at first became surcharged with this spirit because of their many reactions. They have been obeying the behests of spiritual impulse, working in war gardens, eliminating luxuries, purchasing bonds, contributing to benevolent enterprises, until democracy is their ruling passion. Every effort a man puts forth in the interest of humanity has a reflex influence upon his inner self and he experiences a spiritual expansion. So it has come to pass that men and women are doing two, three, or ten times the amount of work they did in the past and doing it better. Their aroused and enlarged spiritual impulses are the enginery that is driving their minds and bodies forward into virgin territory, into new and larger enterprises, and thus into a wider, deeper realization of their own capabilities. So the leaven of democracy is working through difficulties of surpassing obduracy and resolving situations that seemed, in the past, to be beyond human achievement. And of democracy it may be said, as of Dame Rumor of old, "She grows strong by motion and gains power by going. Small at first through fear, she presently raises herself into the air, she walks upon the ground and lifts her head among the clouds." On the side of democracy, at any rate, it would seem that education is beginning to find its way again.

In the thinking of most people democracy is a form of government; but primarily it is not this at all. Rather it is a spiritual attitude. The form of government is an outward manifestation of the inward feeling. Our ancestors held democracy hidden in their hearts as they crossed the ocean long before it became visible as a form of government. The form of government was [99]inevitable, seeing that they possessed the feeling of democracy, and that they were journeying to land in obedience to the dictates of this feeling. In education for democracy the form of government is an after-consideration; that will come as a natural sequence. The chief thing is to inoculate the spirits of people with a feeling for democracy. This germ will grow out into a form of government because of the unity of feeling and consequent thinking. When this spiritual attitude is generated, not only does the form of government follow, but people meet upon the plane of a common purpose and give expression to their inner selves in like movements. They come to realize that, in a large way, each one is his brother's keeper. They are drawn together in closer sympathy and good-will; artificial barriers disappear; and they all become interested in the common good. Their interests, purposes, and activities become unified, and life becomes better and richer. Actuated by a common impulse, they exemplify what Kipling says in his *Sons of Martha*:

> Lift ye the stone or cleave the wood to make a path more fair or flat,
>
> Lo, it is black already with blood some Son of Martha spilled for that,
>
> Not as a ladder from Earth to Heaven, not as an altar to any creed,
>
> But simple Service, simply given, to their own kind, in their common need.

As Dr. Henry van Dyke well says, "It is the silent ideal in the hearts of the people which molds character and guides action."

It will be admitted without qualification that the school, when well administered, constitutes a force that a altogether favorable to the development of the spirit [100]of democracy, and no one will deny that democracy is a worthy goal toward which the activities of the school should be directed. It is easy to see just how geography, for instance, may be made a means to this end. The members of the class represent many conditions of society, but in the study of geography they unite in a common enterprise and have interests in common. Thus their spirits merge and, for the time, they become unified in a common quest. They become coordinates and confederates in this quest of geography, and the spirit of democracy expands in an atmosphere so favorable to growth. These pupils may differ in race, in creed, or in color, but these differences are submerged in the zeal of a common purpose. Lines of demarcation are obliterated and they are drawn together because of their thinking and feeling in unison. The caste system does not thrive in the geography class and snobbery languishes. The pupils have the same books, the same assignments, the same teacher, and share alike in all the privileges and pleasures which the class provides. Their grades are given on merit, with no semblance of discrimination. In short, they achieve the democratic attitude of spirit by means of the study of geography.

If the teacher holds democracy in mind, all the while, as the goal of endeavor, she will find abundant opportunities to inculcate and develop the democratic ideal. By tactful suggestion she directs the activities of the children into channels that lead to unity of purpose. Where help is needed, she arranges that help may be forthcoming. Where sympathy will prove a solace, sympathy will be given, for sympathy grows spontaneously in a democratic atmosphere. Books, pictures, and flowers come forth as if by magic to bear their [101]kindly messages and to render their appointed service. By the subtle alchemy of her very presence, the teacher who is deeply imbued with the spirit of democracy fuses the spirits of her pupils and causes them to blend in the pursuit of truth. Thus she brings it to pass that the spirit of democracy dominates the school and each pupil comes to feel a sense of responsibility for the well-being of all the others. So the school achieves the goal of democracy by means of the studies pursued, and the pupils come to experience the altruism, the impulse to serve, and the centrifugal urge of the democratic spirit.

[102]

Chapter Thirteen

Serenity

Return to Table of Contents

Serenity does not mean either stolidity or lethargy; far otherwise. Nor does it mean sluggishness, apathy or phlegmatism; quite the contrary. It does mean depth as opposed to shallowness, bigness as opposed to littleness, and vision as opposed to spiritual myopia. It means dignity, poise, aplomb, balance. It means that there is sufficient ballast to hold the ship steady on its way, no matter how much sail it spreads. When we see serenity, we are quite aware of other spiritual qualities that foster it and lift it into view. We know that courage is one of the hidden pillars on which it rests and that sincerity contributes to its grace and charm. It is a vital crescent quality as staunch as the oak and as graceful as the rainbow. It evermore stands upon a pedestal, and a host of devotees do it homage. It is as majestic and beautiful as the iceberg but as warm-hearted as love. It has reserve, and yet it attracts rather than repels. A thousand influences are poured into the alembic of the spirit, and serenity issues forth in modest splendor.

This quality of the spirit both betokens and embodies power, and power governs the universe. Its power is not that of the storm that harries and devastates, but rather that of the sunshine that fructifies, purifies, chastens, and ripens. It does not rush or crash into a situation but steals in as quietly as the dawn, without noise or bombast, and, by its gentle influence, softens asperities and wins a smile from the face of sorrow, or discouragement, or anger. Its presence transforms discord into harmony, irradiates gloom, and evokes rare [103]flowers from the murky soil of discontent. Whatever storms may rage elsewhere and whatever darkness may enshroud, it ever keeps its place as the center of a circle of calm and light. It is Venus of Milo come to life, silently distilling the beauty and splendor of living. In its presence harshness becomes gentleness, hysteria becomes equanimity, and sound becomes silence. From its presence vaunting and vainglory and arrogance hasten away to be with their own kind. By its power, as of a miracle, it changes the dross into fine gold, the grotesque into the seemly, the vulgar into the pure, the water into wine. Into the midst of commotion and confusion it quietly moves, saying, "Peace, be still!" and there is quiet and repose. Like the sun-crowned summit of the mountain, it stands erect and sublime nor heeds the cloudy tumult at its feet. In the school, the teacher who exemplifies and typifies this quality of serenity is never less than dignified but, withal, is never either cold or rigid. Children nestle about her in their affections and expand in her presence as flowers open in the sunshine. She cannot be a martinet nor, in her presence, can the children become sycophants. Her very presence generates an atmosphere that is conducive to healthy growth. There is that impelling force about her that draws people to her as iron filings are drawn to the magnet. Her smile stills the tumult of youthful exuberance and when the children look at her they gain a comprehensive definition of a lady. Her poise steadies the children in all the ramifications of their work, her complete mastery of herself wins their admiration, and her complete mastery of the situation wins their respect. They become inoculated with her spirit and make daily advances toward the goal of serenity. Knowledge is her [104]meat and drink and, through the subtle alchemy of sublimation, her knowledge issues forth into wisdom. She does not pose, for her simplicity and sincerity have no need of artificial garnishings. Her outward mien is but the expression of her spiritual power, and when we contemplate her we know of a truth that education is a spiritual process.

To the teacher without serenity, the days abound in troubles. She is nervous, peevish, querulous, and irritable, and her pupils become equally so. She thinks of them as incorrigibles and tells them so. To her they seem bad and she tells them so. Her animadversions reflect upon their parents and their home life as well as themselves and she takes unction to herself by reason of her strictures. Her spiritual ballast is unequal to the sail she carries and her craft in consequence careens and every day ships water of icy coldness that chills her pupils to the heart. She has knowledge, indeed much knowledge, but she lacks wisdom, hence her knowledge becomes weakness and not power. She has spiritual hysteria which manifests itself in her manner, in her looks, and in her voice. Her spiritual strength is insufficient for the load she tries to carry and her path shows uneven and tortuous. She nags and scolds in strident tones that ruffle and rasp the spirits of her pupils and beget in them a longing to become whatever she is not. She is noisy where quiet is needful; she causes disturbance where there should be peace; and she disquiets where she should soothe. She may have had training, but she lacks education, for her spiritual qualities show only chaos. The waters of her soul are shallow and so are lashed into tumult by the slightest storm. She lacks serenity.

The test of a real teacher is not whether she will be [105]good *to* the children but, rather, whether she will be good *for* the children, and these concepts are wide apart. If our colleges and normal schools could but gain the notion that their function is to prepare teachers who will be good *for* children they might find occasion to modify their courses radically. Unless she has serenity the teacher is not good for children, for serenity is one of the qualities which they themselves should possess as the result of their school experience and it is not easy for them to achieve this quality if the teacher's example and influence are adverse. We test prospective teachers for their knowledge of this subject and that, when, in reality, we should be trying to determine whether they will be good for the pupils. But we have contracted the habit of thinking that knowledge is power and so test for knowledge, thinking, futilely, that we are testing for power. We judge of a teacher's efficacy by some marks that examiners inscribe upon a bit of paper, "a thing laughable to gods and men." She may be proficient in languages, sciences, and arts and still not be good for the children by reason of the absence of spiritual qualities. None the less, we admit her to the school as teacher when we would decline to admit her to the hospital as nurse. We say she would not be good for the patients in the hospital but nevertheless accept her as the teacher of our children.

In Ephesians we read, "But the fruit of the Spirit is love, joy, peace, longsuffering, gentleness, goodness, faith, meekness, temperance," and such an array of excellent spiritual qualities should attract the attention of all the agencies that have to do with the preparation of teachers. We need only to make a list of the opposites of these qualities to be convinced that the [106]teacher who possesses these opposites would not be good for the children. Now serenity embodies all the foregoing excellent qualities and, therefore, the teacher who has serenity has a host of qualities that will make for the success and well-being of her pupils. Again, quoting from Henderson: "My whole point is that these spiritual qualities in a boy are infinitely more important to his present charm and future achievement than any amount of academic training, than the most complete knowledge of reading, writing, arithmetic, history, geography, grammar, spelling, classics, and natural science. For charm and achievement are of the Spirit. It is very clear, then, that we ought to make these spiritual qualities the major end of all our endeavor during those wonderful years of grace; and that we ought to allow the intellectual development, up to fourteen years at least, to be a by-product, valuable and welcome certainly, but not primarily sought after. In the end we should get much the larger harvest of intellectual power, and much the larger man."

We cannot hope to achieve the reconstructed school until our notion of teaching and teachers has been reconstructed. When we secure teachers who have education and not mere knowledge, we may begin to hope. We must look to the colleges and normal schools to furnish such teachers. If they cannot do so, our schools must plod along on the path of tradition without hope of finding the better way. There are faint indications, however, here and there, that the colleges and normal schools are beginning to stir in their sleep and are becoming somewhat aware of their opportunities and responsibilities. We shall hail with acclaim the glad day when they come to realize that the preparation of teachers for their work is a task of [107]large import and goes deeper than facts, and statistics, and theories, and knowledge. If they furnish a teacher who has the quality of serenity, we shall all be fully alive to the fact that that quality is the luscious and nutritious fruitage of scholarship, of wide knowledge, of much reading, of deep meditation, and keen observation. But these elements, either singly or in combination, are but veneer unless they strike their roots into the spiritual nature and are thus nourished into spiritual qualities. Excavating into serenity, we shall discover the pure gold of scholarship; we shall find knowledge in great abundance; we shall find the spirit of the greatest and best books; and we shall come upon the cloister in which meditation has done its perfect work.

The machine that is run to the extreme limit of its capacity splutters, sizzles, hisses, and quivers, and finally shakes itself into a condition of ineffectiveness. But the machine that is run well within the limits of its capacity is steady, noiseless, serene, effective, and durable. So with people. The person who essays a task that is beyond his capacity is certain to come to grief and to create no end of disturbance to himself and others before the final catastrophe. If the steam-chest or boiler is not equal to the task, wisdom and safety would counsel the installation of a larger one. Here is one of the tragedies of our scheme of education. The spirit is the power-plant of all life's operations and in this plant are many boilers. Instead of calling more and more of these into action, we seem intent upon repressing them and thus we reduce the capacity of the plant as a whole. When we should be lighting or replenishing the fires under the boilers of imagination, initiative, aspiration, and reverence, we [108]spend our time striving to bank or quench these fires and in playing and dawdling with the torches of arithmetic, grammar, and history with which we should be kindling the fires. Thus we diminish the power of the plant while life's activities are calling for extension and enlargement. We seem to be trying to train our pupils to work with one or but few boilers when there are scores of them available if only we knew how to utilize them.

Hence, it must appear that reserve-power and serenity are virtually synonymous. The teacher who has achieved serenity never uses all the power at her command and, in consequence, all her actions are easy, quiet, and even. She is always stable and never mercurial or spasmodic. She encounters steep grades, to be sure, but with ease and grace she applies a bit more power from her abundant supply and so compasses the difficulty without disturbing the calm. She is fully conscious of her reservoir of power and can concentrate all her attention upon the work in hand. The ballast in the hold keeps the mast perpendicular and the sails in position to catch the favoring breeze. We admire and applaud the graceful ship as it speeds along its course, giving little heed to the ballast in the hold that gives it poise and balance. But the ballast is there, else the ship would not be moving with such majestic mien. Nor was this ballast provided in a day. Rather it has been accumulating through the years, and bears the mark of college halls, of libraries, of laboratories, of the auditorium, of the mountain, the ocean, the starry night, of the deep forest, of the landscape, and of communion with all that is big and fine.

Socrates drinking the hemlock is a fitting and inspiring illustration of serenity. In the presence of [109]certain and imminent death he was far less perturbed than many another man in the presence of a pin-prick. And his imperturbability betokened bigness and not stolidity. While his disciples wept about him, he could counsel them to calmness and discourse to them upon immortality. He wept not, nor did he shudder back from the ordeal, but calm and masterful he raised the cup to his lips and smiled as he drank. His serenity won immortality for his name; for wherever language may be spoken or written, the story of Socrates will be told. History will not permit his name to be swallowed up in oblivion, not alone because he was the victim of ignorance and prejudice but also because his serenity, which was the offspring and proof of his wisdom, did not fail him and his friends in the supreme test. It is not a slight matter, then, to set up serenity as one of the goals in our school work. Nor is it a slight matter for the teacher to show forth this quality in all her work and so inspire her pupils to follow in her footsteps.

We hope, of course, that the boys and girls of our schools may attain serenity so that, even in their days of youth, urged on as they are by youthful exuberance, they may be orderly, decorous, and kindly-disposed. We would have them polite, as a matter of course, but we would hope that their politeness may be a part of themselves and not a mere accretion. They will have joy of life, but so does their teacher who is possessed of serenity. Joy is not necessarily boisterous. The strains of music are no less music because they are mellow. We would have our young people think soberly but not solemnly. And when all our people, young and old, reach the goal of serenity they will extol the teachers and the schools that showed them the way.

[110]

Chapter Fourteen

Life

Return to Table of Contents

Finally, we come to the chief among the goals, which is life itself. In fact, life is the super-goal. We study manual arts, science, and language that we may achieve the goals of integrity, imagination, aspiration, and serenity, and these qualities we weave into the fabric of life. Upon the spiritual qualities we weave into it, depend the texture and pattern of this fabric and the generating and developing of these qualities and the weaving of them into this fabric—this we call life. When we look upon a person who is well-conditioned and whose life is well-ordered, in body, in mind, and in spirit, we know, at once, that he possesses integrity, initiative, a sense of responsibility, reverence, and other high qualities that compose the person as we see him. We do not reflect upon what he knows of history, of geography, or of music, for we are taking note of an exemplification of life. Indeed, the presence or absence of these qualities determines the character of the person's life. Hence it is that life is the supreme goal of endeavor. Life is a composite and the crown-piece of all the qualities toward which we strive by means of arithmetic and grammar—in short, of all our activities both in school and out.

One of our mistakes is that we confuse life and lifetime, and construe life to mean the span of life. In this conception the unit of measurement is so large that our concept of life evaporates into a vague generalization. Life is too specific, too definite for that. The quality of life may better be measured and tested in one-hour periods of duration. When the clock strikes [111]nine, we know that in just sixty minutes it will strike ten. In the space of those sixty minutes we may find a cross-section of life. In a single hour we may experience a thousand sensations, arrive at a thousand judgments, and make a thousand responses to things about us. In that hour we may experience joy, sorrow, love, hate, envy, malice, sympathy, kindliness, courage, cowardice, pettiness, magnanimity, egoism, altruism, cruelty, mercy—a list, in fact, that reaches on almost interminably. If we only had a spiritual cyclometer attached to us, when the clock strikes ten we should have an interesting moment in noting the record. Only in some such way may each one of us gain a true notion of what his own life is. The one-hour period is quite long enough for a determination of the spiritual attitude and disposition of the individual.

It is no small matter to achieve life, big, full, round, abounding, pulsating life; but it is certainly well worth striving for. Some one has defined sin as the distance between what one is and what he might have been; and this distance measures his decline from the sphere of life to which he had right and title. For life is a sphere, seeing that it extends in all directions. Its limits are conterminous with the boundaries of time and space. The feeble-minded person has life, but only in a very restricted sphere. He eats; he drinks; he sleeps; he wanders in narrow areas; and that is all. His thinking is weak, meager, and fitful. To him darkness means a time for sleeping, and light a time for eating and waiting. He produces nothing either of thought or substance, but is a pensioner upon the thinking and substance of others. His eyesight is strong and his hearing unimpaired; but he neither sees nor hears as normal persons do, because his spirit is incapable of [112]positive reactions, and his mind too weak to give commands to his bodily organs at the behest of the spirit. In the language of psychology, he lacks a sensory foundation by which to react to external stimuli.

In striking contrast is the man whose sphere of life is large, whose spirit is capable of reacting to the orient and the occident, to height and depth, and whose mind flashes across the space from the dawn to the sunset, and from nadir to zenith. Space is his playground, and his companions are the stars. Such a man feels and knows more life in an hour than his antithesis could feel and know in a century. To his spirit there are no metes and bounds; it has freedom and strength to make excursions to the far limits of space and time. Life comes to him from a thousand sources and in a thousand ways because he is able to go out to meet it. There has been developed in him a sensory foundation by which he can react to every influence the universe affords, to light and shadow, to joy and sorrow, to the near and the far, to the then and the now, to the lowly and the sublime, and to the finite and the Infinite. He has a big spirit, which is first in command; he has a strong, active mind, which is second in command; and he has a loyal company of bodily organs that are able and willing to obey and execute commands.

To such a man we apply all the epithets of compliment and commendation which the language yields and cite him as an exemplification of life at high tide, of life in its supreme fullness and splendor. The knowledge of the world comes to his doors to do his bidding; before him the arts and sciences make their obeisance; and wisdom is his pillar of cloud by day and his pillar of fire by night. Therefore we call him educated; we [113]call him a man of culture; we call him a gentleman; and all because he has achieved life in abundant measure. Having imagination, he is able to peer into the future, anticipate world movements, and visualize the paths on which progress will travel. Having initiative as his badge of leadership, he is able to rally hosts of men to his standard to execute his behests for civic, national, and world betterment. Having aspiration, he obeys the divine urge within him and moves onward and upward, eager to plant the flag of progress upon the summit that others may see and be stimulated to renewed hope and courage.

And he has integrity, for he is a real man. He has wholeness, completeness, soundness, and roundness. He is an integer and never counts for less than one in any relation of life. He cannot be a mere cipher, for he is dynamic. He rings true at every impact of life, is free from dross and veneer, and is genuine through and through. There was arithmetic, back along the line somewhere, but it has been absorbed in the big quality which it helped to generate and develop. And it is better so. For if he were now solving decimals and square root he would be but a cog and not the great wheel itself. He has grown beyond his arithmetic as he has grown beyond his boyhood warts and freckles, for the larger life has absorbed them. Yet he feels no disdain either for freckles or arithmetic, but regards them as gracious incidents of youth and growth. He cannot read his Latin as he once could, but he does not grieve; for he knows it has not been lost but, in changed form, is enshrined in the heart of integrity.

Again, he has the qualities of thoroughness, concentration, a sense of responsibility, loyalty, and serenity. [114]He is big enough, and true enough both to himself and others, to pursue a straight and steady course. To him, life is a boon, a privilege, an investment, an opportunity, a responsibility, and, therefore, a gift too precious to be squandered or frivoled away. To him, hours are of fine gold and should be seized that they may be fused and fashioned into a statue of beauty. Being loyal to this conception, he moves on from achievement to achievement nor stops to note that fragrant flowers of blessing and benediction are springing forth luxuriantly in his path. His spirit is big with rightness, his brain is clear, his conscience is clean, his eyes look upward, his words are sincere, his thoughts are lofty, his purposes are true, and his acts distill blessings. He is no mere figment of fancy, but rather a noble reality whose prototype may be found on the bench, in the forum, in the study, in the sanctum, in the school and the college, in the factory, on the farm, and in the busy mart.

And, withal, he is a success as a human being. His sincerity is proverbial in all things, both great and small. In him there is nothing of the mystic, the hermit, or the sybarite. He has great joy of life, and this joy is true, honest, and real, and never simulated. He drinks in life at every pore, and gives forth life that invigorates and inspires whomsoever it touches. His laugh is the expression of his wholesome nature; his words are jewels of discrimination; his every sentence bears a helpful message; his fine sense of humor mellows and illumines every situation; and his face always shows forth the light within. Children find delight in his society, and the exuberant vitality of his nature wins for him the friendship of all living creatures. Birds seem to sing for him, and flowers to exhale their [115]odors for his delight. For the influences of birds, flowers, streams, trees, meadows, and mountains are enmeshed in his life. Nature reveals her secrets to him and gives to him of her treasures because he goes out to meet her. Because he smiles at nature she smiles back at him, and the union of their smiles gives joy to those who see.

Moreover, he is a product of the reconstructed school, for this school does already exist, though in conspicuous isolation. But the oasis is accentuated by its isolation in the desert which spreads about it and is the more inviting by contrast. When, as a child, he entered school, the teacher, who was in advance of her time in her conception of the true function of the school, made a close and sympathetic appraisement of his aptitudes, his native dispositions, his daily environment, and the bent of his inherent spiritual qualities. First of all, she won his confidence. Thus he found freedom, ease, and pleasure in her presence. Thus, too, there ensued unconscious self-revelation and nothing in his life evaded her kindly scrutiny. He opened his mind to her frankly and fully, and never after did she permit the closing of the door. Only so could she become his teacher.

She regarded him as an opportunity for the testing of all her knowledge, all her skill, and the full measure of her altruism. Nor was he the proverbial mass of plastic clay to be molded into some preconceived form. Her wisdom and modernity interdicted such a conception of childhood as that. Rather, he was a growing plant, waiting for her skill to nurture him into blossom and fruitage. Some of his qualities she found good; others not. The good ones she made the objects of her special care; the others she allowed to perish from [116]neglect. Her experience in gardening had taught her that, if we cultivate the potatoes assiduously, the weeds will disappear and need not concern us. She discerned in him a tender shoot of imagination and this she nurtured as a priceless thing. She fertilized it with legend, story, song, and myth, and enveloped it in an atmosphere of warmth and joyousness. She led him into nature's realm, that his imagination might plume its wings for greater flights by its efforts to interpret the heart of things that live. Thus his imagination learned to traverse space, to explore sights and sounds his senses could not reach, and to construct for him another world of beauty and delight.

So, too, with the other spiritual qualities. Upon these goals her gaze was fixed and she gently led him toward them. She taught the arithmetic with zest, with large understanding, and in a masterly way, for she was causing it to serve a high purpose. Whatever study she found helpful, this she used as a means with gratitude and gladness. If she found the book ill adapted to her purpose, she sought or wrote another. If pictures proved more potent than books, the galleries obeyed the magic of her skill and yielded forth their treasures. She yearned to have her pupil win the goals before him; everything was grist that came to her mill if only it would serve her purpose. She disdained nothing that could afford nourishment to the spirit of the child and give him zeal, courage, and strength for the upward journey. If more arithmetic was needful, she found it; if more history, she gave it; and if the book on geography was inadequate, she supplemented from libraries or from her own abundant storehouse of knowledge. She dared to deviate from the course of study, if thereby the child might more certainly[117] win the goals toward which she ever looked and worked.

In the boy, she saw a poet, a philosopher, a prophet, an artist, a musician, a statesman, or a philanthropist, and she worked and prayed that the artist in the child might not die but that he might grow to stalwart manhood to glorify the work of her school. In each girl she saw another Ruth, or Esther, or Cordelia, or Clara Barton, or Frances Willard, or Florence Nightingale, or Rosa Bonheur, or Mrs. Stowe, or Mrs. Browning. And her heart yearned over each one of these and strove with power to nourish them into vigorous life that they might become jewels in her crown of rejoicing. She must not allow one to perish through her ignorance or malpractice, for she would keep her soul free from the charge of murder. And in the fullness of manhood and womanhood her pupils achieved the full symphony of life. They had won the goals toward which their teacher had been leading. Their spiritual qualities had converged and become life, and they had attained the super-goal. In the joy of their achievement their teacher repeated the words of her own Teacher, "I am come that they might have life, and that they might have it more abundantly."